The RIVER CAMEL

BRENDA DUXBURY and MICHAEL WILLIAMS

BOSSINEY BOOKS

First published in 1977 as
Along the Camel by
Bossiney Books, St Teath,
Bodmin, Cornwall.
Enlarged, revised edition
published 1987.
Typeset and printed in
Great Britain by Penwell Ltd,
Parkwood, Callington, Cornwall.

ISBN 0 948158 26 3

Plate Acknowledgements

Front cover: Ray Bishop
Ray Bishop: pages 5, 7, 10-15, 20-22, 25-27,
    31, 32, 37-47, 55, 57, 63, 65-72, 74, 76, 81,
    82, 90, 100, 101
George Ellis: pages 17, 61, 64, 80, 88, 93
    94, 96
Royal Institution of Cornwall: page 92
John Watts: pages 29, 48, 51, 85
Ken Duxbury: pages 16, 19, 53
Heather Griffiths: pages 73, 79
Paul Honeywill: page 34
R.W. Hawken: page 24

Acknowledgements

We are indebted to Faber & Faber for the
use of some words from Sir John Betjeman's
Shell Guide *Cornwall;* the Royal Institution
of Cornwall for allowing Heather Griffiths to
work from the original photograph of Prideaux Place; the St Enodoc Golf Club for
Bernard Darwin's description; the editor of
The Guardian for permission to quote two
paragraphs from Raymond Gardner's article
on Padstow May Day; and not least the Padstow Museum for opening its doors out of
season and being so helpful.
    Finally, we sincerely thank local people
who talked to us—and helped to bring the
past back to life. We only hope we have done
those people and this lovely stretch of
Cornwall something like justice.

Front cover: Heather Swain looks down the
Camel estuary.

About the Authors & the Book

Michael Williams, a Cornishman, runs Bossiney Books with his wife Sonia from a cottage and converted barn in North Cornwall—this is their 140th title. His recent titles include *The Moors of Cornwall* and *Paranormal in the Westcountry*.

With her sailor-author husband Ken, Brenda Duxbury lives high above the Camel at St Breward on the edge of Bodmin Moor. She has been editing Bossiney titles for more than ten years, and combines the life of an editor with that of massage therapist.

Brenda Duxbury and Michael Williams collaborated with Colin Wilson in 1979 to produce *King Arthur Country in Cornwall* which remains one of Bossiney's bestsellers.

This is an enlarged and updated version of *Along the Camel* first published in 1977 and out of print for several years. 'We have added a good deal of new material,' the authors say, 'and many of the photographs have been especially taken for this new edition.' They describe the Camel as 'one of the great glories of Cornwall' and explore the river from its source above the town of Camelford all the way to the point where it joins the Atlantic Ocean.

'We hope we have managed to capture the essential quality of the Camel and the people who live—or have lived—close by her.' History and legend, characters as diverse as Sir John Betjeman and healer Nelson Side, railways and sailing, Padstow 'Obby 'Oss and the North Cornwall Museum are only some of the facets on this exploration.

The River Camel

The Camel is one of the great glories of Cornwall.

The plain fact is rivers are among the most graceful of characters in all Nature. Somehow the best scenery is always where a river flows. Wise perceptive Ronald Duncan once reflected that rivers 'seem to lend the country through which they flow a vitality engendered from their own movement, and a serenity reflected from their quiet pools. A river suggests affluence and assures fertility.'

All of which is true in relation to the Camel and the Cornish landscape. The Camel is a rare slice of Cornish magic, linking the countryside to the sea.

Outside and beyond all that, history and legend intensify the mystery and the magic of the Camel. Yet, despite the mystery and the magic, and perhaps because of it, there is a sense of continuity in Camel Country.

Sarah Foot, in her beautifully crafted *Rivers of Cornwall*, has touched on this subject: '. . . and nowhere has the spirit of Arthur been so revitalised as in Cornwall. People, who made their living in a tough and strenuous manner, in fishing, mining and on the land, used these legends to colour their lives and they do not intend to let them die out . . .

'Now there are fishermen, farmers, potters, miners, boatbuilders and those who cater for the tourist trade who live along the Camel, but those who went before have left their mark—layers of history and legend are spread across the countryside.'

This then is a journey in words and pictures, and, as authors, we have been fortunate to have the company and skills of photographer

The Camel at Rock: '. . . rivers seem to lend the country through which they flow a vitality . . .'

4

Ray Bishop, a man who knows the Camel almost as well as his green Wadebridge garden. Ray is a photographer for all the seasons. Moreover he has been photographing the Camel in her varying moods for more than thirty years and inside these pages are some of his finest photographs. They evoke the spirit of the place. So, in a real sense, Ray is co-author too.

But a few words of warning before we begin our journey. Within the limits of this publication, you cannot produce a comprehensive picture of the great river. To do that, you would need a thousand pages—and still offend by leaving out things of significance.

However, we hope that we have managed to capture the essential quality of the Camel and the people who live—or have lived—close by her.

Why the Camel?

Surely, nothing could be further from the arid desert than this green and seagirt coast of North Cornwall. But in truth this is an apt description of the river, for to a Cornishman *cam* means crooked.

And crooked it is. Flowing south towards Bodmin, the Camel does an unexpected 'U' turn, northwards to the Bristol Channel. Even the estuary strikes due south from seaward, then bends eastwards through a right angle from Padstow before swinging southwards again to Wadebridge.

Twisting its six mile way between sand dunes on one side and green-topped cliffs on the other, on average under half a mile wide, the estuary is always beautiful even on a stormy day—conditions in which Turner, the greatest of British painters, would have produced his most vivid, exciting work. Actually Turner may well have seen it on such a day, for he spent a winter in Cornwall and travelled up the north coast to capture Tintagel and Boscastle on canvas.

The River Camel begins high above the town of Camelford at a spring on Hendraburnick Down, roughly halfway between a quarry and the remains of the manor house of Hendraburnick. Tall grey pylons excepted, it is a primitive landscape, peopled principally by grazing sheep and cattle, its few trees bent by the prevailing winds. A tiny streamlet trickles across this soggy yet harsh landscape, the

*'The history of Padstow has always had a seafaring
flavour' and that is still true today.*

6

An earlier view of Camelford—a town with Camelot connections.

beginning of its tortuous journey to join the Atlantic beyond the Doom Bar.

The character of a locality, like that of a face, is largely moulded by its past. Over the ages, both merchant and invader, missionary and immigrant, have sailed up the Camel. Apart from Hayle near St Ives, it is the only estuary likely to offer refuge in this notoriously ironbound northern coast. What sailor today does not feel a thrill of anticipation on making a landfall at Stepper Point?

No wonder then the Camel Valley has always formed an important routeway to the south coast across the Cornish peninsula, linking with the River Fowey. Since prehistoric times, travellers from Ireland and Wales have by this means avoided the perilous rounding of Land's End, and once on the south coast, could embark again for Brittany, the Continent and even the Mediterranean. And this was not a one-way route, for the lure of tin and copper brought many travellers to Cornwall across the English Channel as well as the Irish Sea.

Such early travellers have left their echoes. Ornamental collars made of Irish gold were discovered at Harlyn near Padstow. Ireland was rich in gold and copper but they needed tin to add that extra cutting edge to bronze daggers and axes. So Bronze Age merchants came trading flat axes and gold ornaments for Cornish tin.

Burial mounds of that time stand out on the skyline, an Iron Age cliff castle guards the mouth of the estuary: both give a dimension to those early people who fished the waters of the Camel and tilled the fields along her banks. Over the centuries man has laboured to mould the landscape.

The Cornish have always earned a hard living from this granite peninsula with its harsh moorland and unyielding cliffs where the endless battle between land and sea is waged. But wherever the land offers a rare sanctuary to the sea, such as this estuary, with each advancing tide a short truce is called.

CAMELFORD

Camelford is the first town we encounter on the Camel—or the last.

A quarter of a century ago, Sir John Betjeman came here and reflected: 'The little town has never been more than a street of unpretentious grey slate houses, the grander being those between the Town Hall (1806) and the bridge over the Camel.'

Since Sir John wrote those words, the town has grown, especially around the edges. But interestingly the main street remains relatively unchanged, judging from old photographs and picture postcards.

In the early 1800s you could buy a wife here for as little as 2s. 6d.— disgruntled husbands made a habit of coming to Camelford Market and disposing of their partners!

We strongly recommend a visit to the North Cornwall Museum. Run by Sally Holden, this lovely old slate-roofed building once housed coaches and wagons. Sally opened it as a museum and art

North Cornwall Museum & Gallery: Left: Sally
Holden operates an early vacuum cleaner and (above)
exhibits from the days of horse-drawn transport.

gallery in 1974, and four years later, she was awarded the Pilgrim Trust award for 'the best small museum in England'. To walk through its door can be a curious experience—like stepping back say fifty or even a hundred years in Cornish time.

Camelford is the home of a remarkable man called Nelson Side—remarkable in that he is a kind of legend in the countryside of North Cornwall. Nelson is a healer with a difference—many of his patients are four-legged: some are domestic pets but the great majority are livestock belonging to farms.

Nelson Side's whole lifestyle changed dramatically in his forties, when he suddenly discovered the power to heal. For more than thirty years he has devoted hundreds of hours to healing sick people

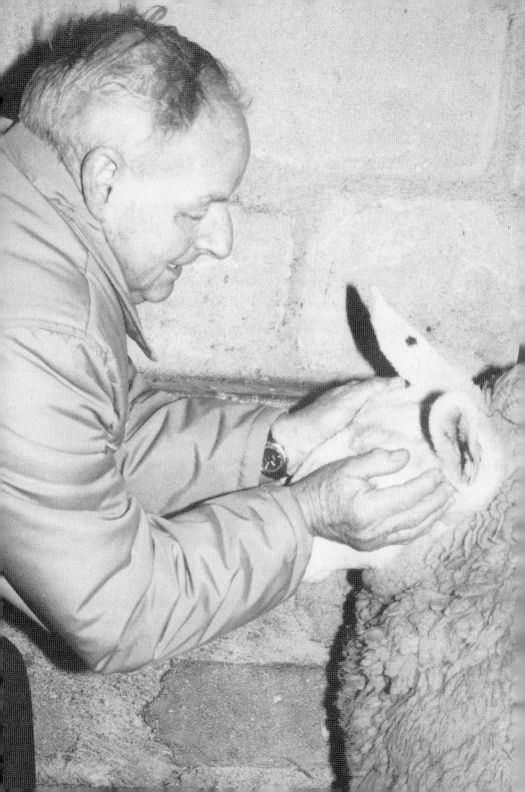

and sick animals. Yet he never takes a penny for all his time and effort. 'If I took money, I feel I might lose the gift,' he says.

SLAUGHTER BRIDGE & ARTHUR

We both remember the times when Camelford Station was in action. Near the old station, a curving road crosses Slaughter Bridge. A visit here is an essential part of any Arthurian tour of Cornwall, for it strides the Camel in its infancy, and the Camel hereabouts is often said to be the site of the Battle of Camlann.

Arthur's fascination is complex, defying easy classification. The Arthurian magnetism is curious: fact and fiction, romance and war, chivalry and tragedy are only some of the ingredients—and beyond them lies the enigma: the impossibility and the probability of it all.

In *King Arthur Country in Cornwall* we have written:

'Malory tells the dramatic story of Arthur's last battle when he was forced to fight his bastard son Mordred who had betrayed him. It was so furious a conflict that in the end only two of the knights of the Round Table were left alive. Arthur knew his time had come. "I am come to mine end," he said and he slew Mordred with his own spear, but the dying traitor raised his sword and struck his father on the head piercing through the helmet to the brain. So Arthur had killed Mordred with his own hands as he had sworn to do.

'Upstream . . . lies the stone, embroidered in moss and strange lettering. It is called Arthur's grave, but it is almost certainly that of another Celtic chieftain.

'And if the stone slab here does commemorate some historic battle, it is more likely to have been one fought in 825 during the Saxon Conquest of Cornwall.'

Nevertheless Camelford, on the strength of name alone, *must* come into any Arthurian reckoning in Cornwall. Its sheer geography puts it clearly on the Arthurian map: only six miles from Tintagel and so close to Slaughter Bridge—and not many miles away on Bodmin Moor are King Arthur's Downs and King Arthur's

Nelson Side: healer with a difference for many of his patients are four-legged.

13

Hall. Camelford then, on the River Camel, has understandably long been a favourite in the search for Camelot.

CAMELFORD TO WADEBRIDGE

As the river leaves Camelford, Bodmin Moor broods over the valley dominated by Roughtor and Brown Willy. Nearer the river, where a small tributary descends from the moor, two rock outcrops known as Devil's Jump stand like sentinels, eyeing each other across the valley.

Another prominent landmark is Advent Church. It is sited roughly three parts of a mile off the Camelford-Bodmin Road—you can see its tall tower from that main road. This is a peaceful sanctuary for anyone on a twentieth-century jaunt across Cornwall, but its geography is curious. It stands quite alone mid fields. There is, however, a quiet power about the place. Happily, too, the bells of Advent still ring across the landscape.

Below the village of St Breward the river cuts right under the edge of the Moor, the valley steep and shrouded in trees. There is always a transitional stage between its birthplace and the lowland areas where the fully-fledged river begins to sense the sea. Here from St Breward the river begins to feel its power, so by the time it reaches Dunmere and turns north to Wadebridge and the coast it is a sizeable river.

A favourite haunt for fishermen it flows through magnificent woods with evocative names like Pencarrow, Helligan and Colquite. Peppered across this landscape above the trees are hillforts, belonging to the Iron Age: Dunmere, Pencarrow and Killibury, possibly the Kellywic of Arthurian history and the birthplace of the king. Even the Romans built a military camp at Nanstallon overlooking the Camel. It is unique in that it is the furthest west that the Roman legions are known to have penetrated.

Such beautiful and historical sites are well worth preserving and one of the groups who keep a watchful eye in this part of the county is the Camel Valley and Bodmin Moor Preservation Society. Its aims are 'to improve, protect and preserve for the benefit of the public, the towns, villages and countryside' within an area covering a major part of the Camel valley and Bodmin Moor.

At one time the railway accompanied the river right from

Wenford to Padstow. Now, in these upper reaches you can only follow its course on foot, the way punctuated by ancient bridges, all with their own stories to tell. Gam, Helland, and Wenford bridges are all crossing places on the Camel of outstanding beauty. Gam, below St Breward, is an original clapper bridge.

As we stood watching the sun slanting through the autumn leaves and glinting on to the weir above Dunmere, we were surprised by the force and the volume of the water. Little wonder then that this power has been harnessed over the years to drive many a mill wheel along the Camel. It's sad that we don't make more use of this free energy today. Indeed one has to look far in Cornwall to find such power still being tapped, which makes Lavethan Mill at Merry Meeting all the more noteworthy, for it has been grinding corn right up to the present day.

Interestingly the tradition of water power has been revived today at Kenningstock Mill where Mike and Inette Austin-Smith, two architects who have imaginatively converted the old mill into a

Slaughter Bridge—legend favours it as the site of the Arthurian Battle of Camlann.

Michael Cardew at the potter's wheel at Wenford and
(left) his son Seth keeps an eye on the kiln.

modern home, use the original mill leat to turn not the traditional wheel but a water turbine which drives a generator to produce a major part of their electricity.

Rivers somehow seem to generate creativity and further down the Camel at Wenford Bridge another traditional skill still thrives. What was it about this idyllic river crossing that enticed Michael Cardew to set up his pottery here in 1939? A decision which led to three generations of his family working as potters at Wenford.

Seth Cardew told us how his father wandered as a boy in Cornwall. At a time when his friends were enjoying the thrills of fast cars, Michael Cardew preferred the pleasures of walking. One day when exploring Dartmoor, he looked westward and saw the ridges of Bodmin Moor, and said 'That's the place for me!' An erudite man, he chose to study pottery and became a pupil of the great Bernard Leach at St Ives. He had already established a considerable reputation when his father died and with a legacy he was able to buy from St Austell Brewery the derelict buildings at Wenford Bridge, once the Wenford Inn.

Seth and his wife Jutta invited us to visit the pottery early on a Sunday morning when the kiln was being fired. Seth had been up at 3 a.m. to light the fire which would take thirty hours to build up to a temperature of 1305 degrees centigrade in the brick kiln. The Cardews still prefer to burn wood rather than change to the convenience of electricity; with wood the through draft modifies the gases and therefore the quality of the glazes.

We asked Seth if there was a family tradition of style. He said that they had continued largely in the style of his father but that shapes were always evolving. Michael Cardew once said that shapes are in continuous need of being made anew, quoting Blake:

> *He who bends to himself a joy*
> *Does the winged life destroy;*
> *But he who kisses the joy as it flies*
> *Lives in eternity's sunrise.*

The Cardew pottery produces a wide range of utensils. Being fired that day was a rather special commission, a 36 inch ewer with jug and basin for a monastery in London for the ritual of washing feet.

Seth works now at his potter's wheel in what used to be the skittle alley of the inn. It is strange to think that Wenford must once have been a busy place. The railhead for unloading sand and taking on granite with quarrymen and railmen enjoying their pint and pasty across the road at the pub.

St Breward is a village of many skills and trades—not only producing stone masons for the quarries but also men who have worked the china clay at Stannon across from Alex Tor on the Moor for more than a hundred years.

It was in 1907 that pipelines were laid across the moor from Stannon to new sidings on the railway below Wenford Bridge where thickening tanks and dries were under construction. At one time there were six kilns in operation but in the 1960s English China Clays replaced the kilns with a modern rotary drying complex. Today the output at Wenford Dries or Dryers is approximately 1700 tonnes a week, the clay being used in papermaking and in the paint, rubber and plastics industries.

18

The sun glints through autumn leaves onto the weir at Dunmere—the Camel is now a sizeable river.

The china clay trains have stopped running but one day the sound of a steam train may be heard once again at Wenford. It will be no ghost train for the Bodmin and Wenford Railway Company is planning to reopen the line from Bodmin Road Station—its name now sadly changed to Bodmin Parkway—to Bodmin General and then on to Boscarne Junction. Mr Baker, the secretary of the company, told us these plans. Long term strategy includes the opening of the magical stretch from Boscarne to Wenford along the Camel valley. North Cornwall District Council are involved in the scheme to provide a footpath alongside the railway. The track today is used by people for walking although there is no general right of way along the whole length. But it has been possible for some years to walk the length of the railway from Padstow to Wadebridge and Cornwall County Council have now extended the Camel Trail all the way to Boscarne Junction.

Left: View from the railcar window near Boscarne Junction just before the line closed. Above: The line continued to Padstow running alongside the estuary.

It is interesting to discover that the Wadebridge to Wenford railway is one of the oldest in the country. Perhaps it is not so strange when one recalls that Cornwall is the homeland of Richard Trevithick—and that Cornish engineers over the years have been fired and inspired by the needs of mines and quarries, rail and water transport.

It was in 1831 that a local landowner, Sir William Molesworth, employed Roger Hopkins to make a survey for a railway from Wadebridge to Wenford Bridge with branches from Dunmere to Bodmin and Grogley to Ruthern Bridge. It opened in 1834, only four years after the pioneering railway linking Stockton and Darlington. Initially the Cornish line had but one engine;

Polbrock Bridge on the romantic stretch of the Camel between Dunmere and Egloshayle.

appropriately called *Camel*. It puffed its way, bringing china clay and granite from the moor and taking sea sand inland from the estuary.

It was not until 1887-8 that the link was made from Bodmin Road to Boscarne through Bodmin General, and Wadebridge was connected with the main line. In 1895 the North Cornwall line from Launceston and Delabole joined at Sladesbridge and in 1899 continued to Padstow carrying the famed 'Atlantic Coast Express'.

Railway journeys in those early days of steam were adventurous with frequent breakdowns and engines being hauled home by horses. Trains stopped anywhere to load and unload. Once a train halted to allow a passenger to recover her purse! A colourful character of the line was Superintendent Hays Kyd, famed for his cocoa and ale tickets, given to the staff in lieu of overtime, the rates of pay being sixpence an hour. Another personality was Samuel Worth who joined as a lookout man. He rode on the front of the engine, opening gates and keeping the track free from straying animals. He worked on the line for six decades, retiring at the age of eighty.

Passenger trains did not run on the Boscarne Wenford section though they were sometimes conveyed in goods trains, especially for outings on high days and holidays when excursion coaches were added.

Today the line is silent, felled by the Beeching axe. The motor car has beaten it, causing more and more chaos on the roads at the height of the holiday season. The 28 January 1967 marked the end of an era when the last passenger train ran from Wadebridge after 132 years of service.

Since then the station at Wadebridge, once the busy headquarters of the railway company, has stood empty. Now a housing estate has consumed the station yard, and plans are evolving to convert the station building into the John Betjeman Centre. The man behind the scheme is Dr Kinsman Barker who is particularly concerned with the care of the elderly. The building will include a Betjeman library and exhibition, featuring the Poet Laureate, a hall, a dayroom and craft workshop.

Sir John Betjeman concerned himself much with railways and stations. He must have disembarked here at Wadebridge many times en route for his home at Trebetherick, so it is fitting this station should now become a living memorial.

EGLOSHAYLE

Egloshayle in the Cornish language means the 'church on the estuary'.

Times were when the river overflowed its banks at the highest tides and rose to the doorsteps of the cottages. Canoes have even been paddled up the Egloshayle road. Since then the river has been restrained by an embankment which incidentally makes an attractive walk. Marshland has been transformed into a recreation area and park with tennis courts, a bowling green and cricket ground.

Minor County matches have been played here at Egloshayle—in

Cricket under the watchful eye of Egloshayle Church—
Wadebridge have won the Cornish championship twice.
Left: Bill Murphy—an outstanding player.

1986 Cornwall played Canada on the ground. Over the years, and at their best, Wadebridge have been a great force in East Cornwall cricket, having appeared in as many as ten finals between the years 1957 and 1973, winning the Cornish championship twice and sharing it once with Truro.

An outstanding cricketer for the club was Yorkshireman Bill Murphy, who also played for Wadebridge Football Club, and excelled on the golf course. Bill Murphy scored thousands of runs for Wadebridge and took a rich harvest of wickets. A right-hand batsman, in the correct Yorkshire mould, he also rendered outstanding service to Cornwall, scoring four centuries for the county club, including a magnificent 175 against Dorset at Penzance.

Egloshayle Church, pleasantly set, overlooks the river. This splendid old building was rebuilt by the enterprising cleric Loveybond round the time of the bridge construction at

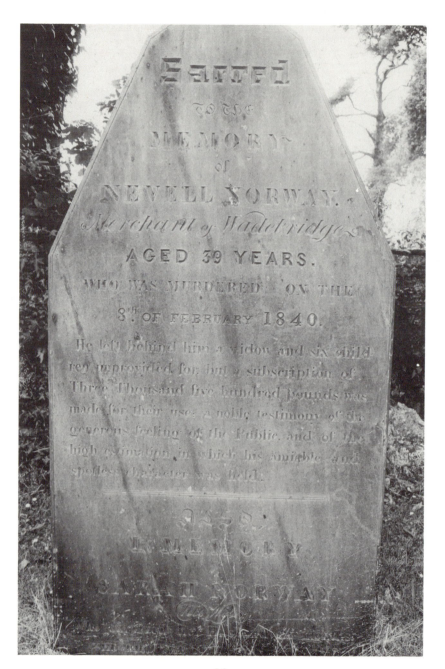

Sacred
To the
MEMORY
of
NEWELL NORWAY.
Merchant of Wadebridge
AGED 39 YEARS.
WHO WAS MURDERED ON THE
8TH OF FEBRUARY 1840.

He left behind him a widow and six child
ren unprovided for, but a subscription of
Three Thousand five hundred pounds was
made for their use; a noble testimony of the
generous feeling of the Public, and of the
high estimation in which his amiable and
spotless character was held.

ALSO
IN MEMORY
of
SARAH NORWAY

Egloshayle Church on the banks of the Camel and (left) the headstone commemorating Nevell Norway, murdered on the road from Bodmin.

Wadebridge. Thomas Loveybond's church is basically fifteenth-century with traces of earlier work. Unplastered walls give a rugged air; as do the two aged Celtic crosses by the south porch. Other items worth seeing are the font, belonging to the Transitional-Norman era and a modern screen which blends beautifully with the lovely pre-Reformation pulpit—one of only two stone pulpits in Cornwall. On the shield decorating the door to the tower, which was built of stone left over from the bridge, you can still trace the inscription 'I love ye bond'—indicating the builder of the tower.

Egloshayle churchyard is interesting for anyone curious about the Supernatural, for there is a tradition that when the moon is bright, you will see a ghostly white rabbit. This four-legged spirit is said to be followed by another: two legged and headless—a man, who disbelieving the existence of a ghost, tried to shoot the white rabbit, only to be found soon after dead among the graves.

27

This story has been well described in 1897 by Arthur Norway, author of *Highways and Byways in Devon and Cornwall*, but the story is still told today in the town.

We have heard it from as many as three Wadebridge residents. The truth is, one encounters less cynicism about the Supernatural in Cornwall than in many other places. Celtic ancestry perhaps? Or maybe mining and fishing, one-time great Cornish industries, had more than their share of tragedy. Thus omens and a belief in the magical assumed a special significance in everyday life. Even today charming and spiritual healing are practised extensively.

In the churchyard you will find also the grave of Nevell Norway, from the same Norway family—as was Neville Shute, the famous novelist. He was murdered not far up the road by the Lightfoot brothers, James and William, on his way home from Bodmin Market in February 1840. Public sympathy, as you can see from the details on the grey headstone, was such that over £3,000 was raised for his widow and her six children.

This crime—and a mass of other interesting stories are to be found in Baring Gould's *Cornish Characters and Strange Events*, published in 1908. And astonishingly this murder was to have a Supernatural postscript. Many people believe dreams foretell. Some think though they can only be accurately interpreted in reverse. One man, who would not have shared this reverse theory, was Edmund Norway, brother of the murder victim. That very night aboard a merchant ship bound for Cadiz, he dreamt with uncanny accuracy.

So vivid was the dream that Edmund, on waking wrote about it, incredibly giving a number of 'facts' about his brother's murder. At their trial the Lightfoot brothers confessed they had twice shot at Norway, and twice the pistol had failed to function. They had then struck him from his saddle and with several blows killed him—all of which Edmund had 'seen' in his dream. Both men were subsequently hanged at Bodmin Gaol, when a large crowd of spectators travelled by a special railway excursion from Wadebridge.

THE BRIDGE

Wadebridge, standing at the head of the Camel Estuary, got its name from the Old English word meaning a ford, or possibly the Latin *vadum.*

*An aerial view of Wadebridge standing at the head of
the Camel estuary.*

By tradition the ford here was so dangerous that a chapel was
erected on each bank enabling travellers on one side to pray for a
safe crossing, and on the other to offer up thanks. Around 1470, the
Vicar of Egloshayle, Thomas Loveybond, raised money to build the
much-needed bridge, but when work was underway difficulties were
encountered—a matter of finding sufficiently strong foundations for
the piers. Legend—and there is no shortage of legendary
explanation in North Cornwall—says the problem was solved by
building on wool-packs.

The bridge, originally 320 feet long and a mere nine feet wide with
seventeen Gothic arches, had angles over each pier as refuge for the

pedestrians against the horse-drawn and ridden traffic. In 1852-3 the bridge was widened a matter of three feet on each side by the building of granite segmental arches thrust out between the cutwaters. There was further widening during 1962-3 when commendable care was shown in preserving its character and appearance.

Thus Wadebridge can proudly boast a 500-year-old bridge in constant use, said by some to be the finest of its kind in Britain. Carew, whose *Survey of Cornwall* gives us a picture of the county in Elizabethan times, certainly rated it 'the longest, the strongest and the fairest that the shire can muster'.

The bridge has had its macabre phases. Times were when the severed heads of criminals were displayed on the parapets, and in 1577 parts of the tortured body of Cuthbert Mayne were suspended from the central arch as a warning to all Papists. During the reign of the first Elizabeth, it was against the law of the land to openly celebrate Mass; and Catholics were forced to take Mass and hear sermons from priests whom they hid in their homes. Mayne, a 33-year-old seminary priest sent from the Continent in disguise, was a chaplain at Golden near Probus. But he was discovered and dragged to notorious Launceston Castle. There he suffered the horror of execution for high treason in Launceston market square, his body being torn to pieces while he was still alive. His torso, cut into four sections, was taken to Wadebridge and three other places and put on public display by the authorities as a warning to others.

All that remains of the priest, who was canonized in 1970, is the top half of his skull which is carried in the Roman Catholic procession each year at Launceston Castle.

During the Civil War, none less than Oliver Cromwell came with 1500 Roundheads to take command of the bridge. With columns of well-trained horses and disciplined men, they must have made an impressive sight. 'If you choose Godly, honest men to be Captains of Horse,' said Cromwell, 'honest men will follow them. I would rather have a plain russet-coated captain that knows what he fights for and loves what he knows, than what you call a gentleman and nothing else.'

Wadebridge can boast a 500-year-old bridge in constant use, built around 1470 by Thomas Loveybond, Vicar of Egloshayle.

So when you walk or drive across the 320 feet of bridge you are literally travelling across a piece of history.

WADEBRIDGE

Gone are the sailing ships. Even in this century they came up to Wadebridge, and you can still see the ancient wharves and quays below the bridge. 'When the tide is out,' Norway wrote of Wadebridge, 'it is as though the town has lost its soul.' And, of course, in Norway's day, the Camel was less silted with sand and mud.

If you stand on the bridge waiting for the rising tide to float the gaggle of boats anchored in midstream, you might be lucky enough to see the flood tide advancing as a small wave—or 'bore'. Carew described it rather more romantically: 'The salt water leaving Padstow floweth up into the country that it may embrace the river Camel, and having performed this natural courtesy, ebbeth away again to yield him the freer passage, by which means they both undergo Wade bridge.'

It is easy to imagine the merchants of Wadebridge alerted by the bore eagerly awaiting the first masts to hove in sight around the bend in the river. In the early 1800s there were about thirty barges carrying sand, coal and other merchandise from Padstow to Wadebridge and further upriver. Farmers, from as far away as Michaelstow and Blisland, bought sand for their fields from depots at Clapper and Sladesbridge. The river must have been very busy and trade thriving, for a plan was mooted to build a canal from Polbrock above Wadebridge to link with the Fowey near Lostwithiel.

In addition to barges at this time it was nothing for a dozen or so coastal schooners and smacks to come up on the spring tide discharging cargoes and taking on corn, granite, china clay and iron ore.

But with the coming of the railway to Padstow in 1899, there was a great decline in river traffic; much of the sand was taken by rail.

Wadebridge Town Hall clock photographed in the 1950s.

This sand from the bed of the estuary downstream is still valued by farmers for its lime content. Originally, barges would dry out on the sandbanks, the bargees shovelling the sand directly into their holds. With the rising tide they would pole upstream to Wadebridge or tie up alongside the landing stages of riverside farms and unload. But today the sand is sucked up from the bottom of the estuary by dredgers and taken by road from Padstow.

There have always been developments along the river and today is no exception, for there are three revolutionary schemes on the drawing board at the present time. Under consideration is a proposal to build a bypass for Wadebridge which would include a bridge over the river near Trevilling Creek below the town. Secondly, Wadebridge Town Council are considering a series of weirs to enable a higher level of water to be maintained to add to the town's amenities. Thirdly, the Camel estuary is one of several estuaries in the country being considered as a possible site for a tidal barrage for the generation of electricity. It would be located below Padstow where the estuary narrows. If these schemes come to fruition they could make as much impact on the area as did the coming of the railway in the last century.

Wadebridge has developed more on its west bank. Some aged slate cottages remain on either side of Molesworth Street, the town's main thoroughfare. Here stands the Molesworth Arms, one of the most interesting buildings in Wadebridge, a sixteenth-century inn with a ghostly legend. Traditionally a phantom coach, drawn by four horses and driven by a headless coachman, careers through the courtyard at midnight on New Year's Eve.

Outside any legendary claim, there have been several inexplicable happenings upstairs at the Molesworth Arms: the ringing of a bell in an empty room, the invisible yet audible rustle of skirts on the stairs leading to the attic, the strange slamming of a door by unseen hands—these are all linked to the murder of a woman in the drawing room, whose body was dragged to the attic. Fact or fiction? There was certainly a dark stain beneath the carpet on that angled floor of the drawing room. The first floor of the Molesworth, in places, gives the feeling of being aboard ship in a heavy swell. The ground and first

At the Molesworth Arms in Wadebridge a phantom coach is driven by a headless coachman through the yard on New Year's Eve.

floors are connected by a lovely curved wooden staircase. First known as *The Fox*, later rechristened *The King's Arms* and then *The Fountain*, it was in 1817 that the landlord John Stephens gave the inn its present name in respect of the family who lived on the other side of the river at Pencarrow. The Molesworths, who once owned the building, were the principal landowners hereabouts, and the family crest is over the main entrance; while in the entrance hall hangs a picture of the Rt. Hon. Sir William Molesworth, Bart, a former Member of Parliament and Secretary of State for the Colonies.

The Molesworth family home, Pencarrow, is just off the Bodmin Road. It is open to the public in the summer months, and we can recommend a visit. A mile-long drive leads you through well-planned woodland with banks of rhododendrons, camellias and hydrangeas—slicing through the banks of an Iron Age hillfort.

The house boasts an impressive entrance on the eastern side, Palladian style. The long south front is capped by a roof of grey Delabole slate from the famous North Cornwall quarry. There are traces of an earlier building, and the back faces a courtyard and cottages.

In the dining room, you will find a valuable collection of family portraits by the great Devon-born painter, Sir Joshua Reynolds. One portrait of special note is that of the Sir John Molesworth who, in 1771, was one of the founders of a banking house in London which eventually became Lloyds Bank.

A few words of warning about Wadebridge. In the peak holiday months, you will find it a busy town, especially on a Monday which is market day. But on three particular days in the calendar you will find it choked with traffic—these dates usually in early June, coinciding with the Royal Cornwall Show.

Under one name or another, the show has been going strong since 1793. It was granted its Royal Charter way back in 1827 and has been permanently based at Wadebridge since 1960. The site, high above the town on the St Columb side, is excellent. The gentle slope of the land and shallow soil combine to allow rapid drainage, so that even after heavy, prolonged rain, the ground dries out remarkably quickly. 1974—the first year that the Royal Cornwall stretched itself to a third day—produced a record attendance figure: 76,147 people. The growth and popularity of the show is vividly reflected in pure facts and figures. Total takings in 1957 from entrance and

Pencarrow, the family home of the Molesworths—
'. . . we can recommend a visit.'

membership fees were £16,000. In 1986 a record attendance of 105,000 paid £248,000.

For more than thirty years Show secretary Albert Riddle has been the key figure, the dynamo behind the growth of the Royal Cornwall into one of the largest agricultural shows in Britain. This is more than a horse and cattle show. There are shows within the show: dogs, poultry, bees, honey, cage birds, fur and pigeon shows—these are only some facets of the Royal Cornwall. Internationally-known show jumpers regularly compete. The Royal Cornwall, for many Cornish people, is an annual pilgrimage—days when town and country meet and mix. Provided you don't mind crowds, it is well worth a visit, giving you real insight into a Westcountry way of life.

*Albert Riddle: Secretary of the Royal Cornwall Show
for more than thirty years.*

ST BREOCK

Nearby is St Breock Churchtown, the parish church romantically nestling at the bottom of a steep valley as if to bridge the stream itself. Tombstones line the slopes on either side. The hamlet is a cluster of a dozen attractive cottages and an old rectory.

Immediately outside the church gate is a charming cottage called 'Chanters'. Once this small house with its own courtyard was the village pub: the Farmers Arms. On Sunday mornings the ringers rang the bells for Matins but instead of listening to the sermon crossed the road for refreshments at the Farmers claiming that ringing was a dry job.

The old Rectory first became one in roughly 1770. Two facts suggest this: one, the general architectural impression is distinctly Georgian; and the other is that a member of the Molesworth family became Rector of the Parish in 1772, probably giving himself a house appropriate to his station. He took an old farmhouse and joined it to a medieval barn. By filling in what was presumably a farmyard he created a large and particularly attractive house, now square, but with the added romance of medieval buttresses.

Successive rectors lived here until 1959 when the Church Commissioners sold it to a London solicitor, insisting in the deeds that the words 'Rectory' or its equivalent should not be used in the name of the house. So it became St Breock Place and was modernised.

Why a church here?

The story goes that it was intended to build the church higher up the slope, but when the masons returned each morning they found the work of the previous day transferred to the bottom of the hill!

The church is dedicated to St Brioc, a Celtic Saint from Wales, who is said to have travelled in Cornwall and on to Brittany where his monastery gave its name to the town of Saint-Brieuc. Probably the church is built on the site of an earlier holy place or chapel, perhaps founded by St Brioc.

Many Cornish churches are dedicated to the Celtic saints who lived around the fifth and sixth centuries AD. Moreover their lives have given us many delightful legends and their names are implanted in the countryside. You cannot move very far along the Camel without being reminded of them in the shape of place names. The majority came as missionaries from Ireland and Wales and landed on the North Cornish coast—where better than the Camel estuary?

St Brychan from Brecon in Wales, was said to have 24 children, all of whom were church founders and missionaries. These prolific and saintly offspring must have sailed up the Camel because they have given their names to so many places on both sides of the river: at St Minver, St Teath, St Endellion, St Issey, St Mabyn and St Tudy, to name just a few. These Celtic saints were not canonised in the sense we know it today. Yet they have great appeal, their stories showing them to be very human and often far from perfect.

But a different form of Christianity was gradually spreading from the Continent through Saxon England starting with the mission of St Augustine in 597. The Saxons finally fought their way to the Tamar eventually defeating the Cornish and controlling the whole peninsula by the tenth century, and naturally the Saxon bishops wished to bring this Celtic church under their rule. So the conquerers granted large areas of land in Cornwall to the Bishop of Sherborne including the manors of Pawton and Burniere, strategic-ally placed on either side of the Camel estuary. Later these were transferred to the new See of Exeter. St Breock is in the manor of Pawton and in medieval times Pawton became a favourite residence of the Bishop of Exeter when travelling in the county. There is little sign today at Pawton farm of the Bishop's palace and deer park, but a large medieval barn may well have been the tithe barn.

The present church of St Breock was built in the thirteenth century and it is unusual in having a long nave, probably because the Bishop held ordinations here. This is really the parish church of Wadebridge for the Camel divides the parish of St Breock from that of Egloshayle. It is natural that the town should grow at the crossing of the river and when Edward II granted the Manor of

St Breock Church nestles romantically at the bottom of a steep valley.

41

Pawton the licence for a market in 1312 Wadebridge was the chosen venue. Perhaps this accounts for the town centre growing up west of the bridge. It was not until 1951 that a parish hall and the chapel of St Mary were built in the town itself in Trevanion Road.

However, Pawton is famous for an earlier monument, the Pawton Quoit. This is a chamber tomb of the megalithic period, over 3500 years ago, and consists of nine upright stone boulders supporting an unusually large capstone. It was originally covered by a mound some seventy feet in length, and it stands on the edge of St Breock Downs, sometimes called Giant's Quoit. Legend has it the stones were thrown to this spot by a giant from Stepper Point at the mouth of the estuary.

Near Pawton at Nanscowe is an inscribed stone, one of several in North Cornwall belonging to the period of our Celtic saints. It reads ULCAGNI FILI SEVERI meaning Ulcagnus son of Severus. Both this stone and the quoit are on private land so you will need permission to view.

THE FLOOD OF 1965

A comparatively recent memorial in St Breock Church records the Wadebridge flood of 1965. Carved in wood it shows the church with flood waters half way up the windows, the dove flying overhead bearing the olive leaf inscribed with the date 1966, when the church was reopened after extensive repairs.

On 14 July 1965, a freak storm burst over Wadebridge spreading up to Port Isaac. From Rock in sunshine the sky up river was darker and more ominous than we have ever seen. Over five inches of rain fell in three and a half hours. Streams overflowed their banks, torrents of water poured down into the town. Hedges and walls, even cars were washed along.

Sam Treglown, former licensee of the Swan Hotel, told us, 'It seems that I have always lived in an area that was liable to flooding. Whilst living in Egloshayle we were regularly flooded by the River Camel at high tides and very heavy rain, and I can remember as a small boy with my brothers and sisters being up all night placing sand bags and brooming back the water at the entrance to Trenant Vale.

'This state of affairs seemed to follow me when I moved to the

Swan Hotel in September 1958. I once saw a photograph of a boat going through the Molesworth Street entrance to the hotel, and many times have been washed out by heavy thunderstorms.

'On St Swithin's day 1965, there was a heavy rainfall, five and a half inches of water in four and a half hours, on high tide. Molesworth Street was a raging river with water going over the tops of cars marooned there, all our bars were flooded to a depth of one and a half feet. My son John, a Cornish wrestler and a big lad, was swept away by the torrent of water and picked up on the level crossing. Thanks to the local fire brigade and help from local council workers we managed to open the bars later in the evening.

'Then in November, 1976, on a Sunday evening just at opening time, a mass of liquid manure from a farm high up in the hill was moving down the street like something out of Quatermass. I was able to get the doors closed and thus avoid a lot of damage, but the "smell" was there for days!

'As you know this hotel is at the lowest level and flooding can easily occur when we have heavy rain and the tide is high, for the surface water cannot get away.'

TREWORNAN

Coming back to the other side of the Camel, beyond Bodieve and Burniere, the River Amble joins it at Trewornan where a dyke has been built across the marshland. Formerly, high tides, combined with heavy rain, swamped the valley meadows and the tide flooded right across the road at Chapel Amble. Until the 1920s barges came up to Amble bringing seaweed, sand and coal and reloading with grain.

Between Trewornan Bridge and Chapel Amble the Cornwall Birdwatching and Preservation Society own in excess of 60 acres of land known as the Walmesley Sanctuary, named after the benefactor Dr R.G. Walmesley, who made the bequest in 1939 of the original 42 acres. The additional parcels of land were ceded to the Society by the families of the adjoining farms as a memorial to a relative, the keenest of bird men, 'Jim' Willcocks.

Following the straightening of the then meandering Amble 25 years ago by the Water Board and the building of the tidal barrage, the wetland nature of the Sanctuary became gradually drier. Now

steps are being taken to overcome this. Pools and scrapes are being opened up leaving stretches of water amid the grassland which will attract more duck, widgeon and teal, and migrating waders and, it is hoped, the return and settling in of wintering white-fronted geese who in past years came in numbers; it was considered an overflow for birds from Slimbridge when the weather was more inclement up-country. Always the geese prepared to leave, as if prompted by some avian calendar, by 11-12 March.

Below the bridge and tidal barrier and commanding a wide view of the upper reaches of the river and so of the feeding and resting areas for both the residents and migrants, members have access to two hides: one at Burniere Point, the second, with access for a wheelchair, looking right across to the western shore of the Camel and about half a mile further downstream. Members record their sightings in the hide log books and these reports are collated and appear in the Mainland County Report, one of two published annually by the Society. To retain the beauty and ecological wealth of the River

Trewornan Bridge where the River Amble joins the Camel. The Bird Sanctuary lies upstream from the bridge.

Camel is of great concern to the Society. Disturbance in whatever form can be monitored.

It must not be forgotten that the Sanctuary is private land.

GENTLE JANE

Gentle Jane almost certainly belongs to legend, not fact. You will find a charming piece of the coastline bearing her name, just beyond Cant Hill.

Hereabouts she lived traditionally in peaceful seclusion—well, almost peaceful seclusion, for one legend tells how roving pirates, hot from a raid and assisting a wounded colleague, seeing her light, hammered on her door demanding food and shelter. But they had no need to demand. Jane opened the door immediately; dressed the wounds of the injured pirate and provided food all round. It is said she never asked a question. To Jane they were God's creatures in need of help . . . and that was enough.

In the words of local writer Eleanor Inglefield: 'I guess Jane had many visitors on wild stormy nights, many hungry mouths to feed, many cuts and wounds to dress with the herbs she grew in her little garden . . . Animals came too. There was the exhausted fox, the starving dog, the wounded bird; all came to her. None was ever refused.'

Nobody knows where or when she died—or where she is supposed to be buried. There is a Court of Camelot quality about her and the intriguing thing is that a lovely stretch of the Camel still bears her name.

PORTHILLY

When the emigrant ships were about to sail from Padstow it was the custom to cross the estuary to St Michael's church to pray for a safe voyage to the New World.

There is a seafaring flavour in that the hassocks in this church

St Michael's Church just above the beach at Porthilly looking down the estuary to Rock.

have been embroidered by members of the Parish depicting ships and boats of all sizes shapes and colours.

There are plenty of Cornish churches in romantic settings, but few can be more romantic than St Michael's at Porthilly on the eastern flank of the estuary. You reach it either by crossing the sands of Porthilly beach or by coming through the farmyard from Porthilly Lane. At high tide the sea laps the churchyard wall.

An unusual feature of St Michael's is the inclination of the north wall, a reminder apparently of how Jesus's head hung on the Cross at Calvary. Twice enlarged, the building was drastically restored in 1865 by the ruthless St Aubyn who erased so much Cornish church history. Here at Porthilly he did, at least, mercifully leave the old roofs and introduce an attractive east window. Before restoration, the then vicar is reputed to have conducted services during heavy rain beneath an opened umbrella. The church is filled with golden light from the plain yellow glass. The porch and vestry are both modern, yet blend delightfully with the old building. Standing in places such as this, we need to remind ourselves of their need for money and every coin in the collecting boxes of our aged churches is some form of insurance that future generations will be able to enjoy them too. The battle against decay is constant—and costly.

Outside stands a noble Celtic cross. One theory is that St Michael's began life as an oratory for a monastic order—probably Bodmin Priory—for you can still see traces of ecclesiastical architecture in Porthilly Farm nearby.

But the name Porthilly means the harbour on the estuary. In fact Norden writing of Porthilly in 1584 saw 'a hamlet and harbor wherin of late yeares ther were few or noe houses, now by their industrious fishinge and the blessing of God, the inhabitantes so increase in abilitye as their prosperitye allureth others to resorte to 'the place and daylie increase the buyldinges, that in few yeares, if they contynue, paynfull and religious, it will grow to be a pretie town.'

However, today the river valley at Porthilly is covered by grassed-over sand dunes; the whole bay is very shallow.

ROCK

The old warehouse on the quay at Rock is a local landmark. There was great distress when the building proved to be dangerous and seemed destined for demolition. However, the Rock Sailing Club fortunately undertook renovations in 1976 keeping the original character. Curiously it seems never to have been a Custom House as often called today—but a store for coal and probably grain.

The Rock Hotel did not escape. It was demolished in 1976. Many will recall with nostalgia the sailing or golfing holidays spent there —others will remember the pints they drank sitting on the wall opposite looking over the estuary.

Rock, in the words of the Poet Laureate Sir John Betjeman, 'has an inn, a Georgian house or two, a Victorian terrace, tamarisks, elms, a wharf and a quay and many detached villas, a few by architects'.

How did Rock get its name? The hamlet is perhaps inappropriately named, for at low tide there is hardly a rock in sight—only a wide, very wide, expanse of golden sand. Some say a solitary rocky outcrop was the answer. Indeed the ferry which has been running

The Quay at Rock before the warehouse was converted into a modern sailing club.

between Rock and Padstow since 1337 was known as Black Rock or Black Tor Passage and belonged to the Duchy Manor of Penmayne. Now operated by the Padstow Harbour Commissioners, who use powerful motor launches, it was originally propelled by oar and sail.

Enid Harvey who lived in Padstow most of her life, coming to Rock in latter years, told us of her father Dr Harvey who practised, like his father-in-law before him, in Padstow, living at Rosehill at the top of the town. He had a surgery in Rock, but if a patient wanted him in an emergency at night, a fire was lit on the beach and he came across by boat—or if it was too rough then it was fourteen miles round the estuary through Wadebridge with horse and trap.

Sand dunes inundate the eastern bank of the estuary from Rock to Daymer Bay, reaching quite far inland. Quantities of sand get shifted around the estuary forming banks which dry out at low tide. As the tide drops; the ferry to Padstow has to make a detour round the Town Bar from Rock and eventually is forced to cross in slightly deeper water off St Saviour's Point.

In recent years great erosion has taken place on the Rock side and a retaining wall of railway sleepers has been constructed to prevent the road from being undercut. It is hard to believe that not many years ago the sand reached nearly to the top of Rock quay, a height today of some fifteen feet.

SAILING AND GOLF

Small wonder that Rock has developed as a sailing centre for the Camel estuary is unique in North Cornwall. No other harbour offers the protection from the Atlantic swell coupled with miles of beautiful dunes, sandy beaches and low grass-topped cliffs. The protection is afforded by the largest sandbank of them all, across the mouth of the estuary—the Doom Bar—thought to be a corruption of Dune Bar. It is here that the fury of the Atlantic swell is broken, leaving much calmer waters inside, which makes it ideal for aquatic sports of all kinds: dinghy sailing, water skiing, fishing and just pottering about in boats. If it is dinghy racing you are after then the Rock Sailing Club offers both menagerie and class racing. They have also acted as hosts for several National Championships. Special areas are designated for water skiing and wind surfing. There is fishing inside the estuary for bass and when a safe crossing of the bar is possible

*An aerial view of Rock with Cassock Hill beyond and
Hawker's Cove and Stepper Point across the estuary.*

mackerel, pollack and flatfish can be hooked from the open sea. All
these activities are controlled by the Harbour Master at Padstow and
his Beachmaster at Rock, who will be pleased to provide all necessary
information.

This estuary is an ideal site for a sailing school and in the last
thirty summers hundreds of novice sailors have learnt the rudi-
ments of this sport. The school has recently been rebuilt and is now
called Ferry Point Sailing Centre. Until 1983 it was part of Westerly
Boats, in whose boatyard at Pityme is an anchor with a wooden
stock dating from Nelson's days. It is thought to be the one used to
hold down an anti-submarine net off Port Quin during the 1914-18
war.

Through its subsidiary, Cornish Crabbers Ltd, Westerly Boats has been successful in bringing the romance of the past into the present. It all started in 1974 when Roger Dongray, a local architect, wanted a traditional boat built in modern materials using today's techniques. After studying the old working boats, he began to rough out the lines of a similar kind of craft, and then asked Westerly Boats to build him one. Thus the first Cornish Crabber was born. In the words of the managing director, Peter Keeling, 'she is a boat with genuine character and has that grace which is associated with topsails and a gaff rig.'

Ken Duxbury, reviewing the boat in *The Sunday Express,* reflected: '. . . anyone standing on the headland as we gybed her round to enter the estuary on top of the flood tide might well have rubbed his eyes and looked long and hard . . . for time could have seemed to slip back fifty or a hundred years.'

Since that time the Crabber has been joined by other traditional designs from Roger Dongray to complete a range from twelve to thirty feet in length. These craft are not only popular with British owners but are exported elsewhere in Europe and to North America.

Apart from sailing, and the general estuary and beach attraction, Rock's other big draw is the St Enodoc Golf Club which has one of the finest, most testing courses in the Westcountry.

Golfing expert Bernard Darwin described the game here as 'eminently natural, amusing and dramatic in a country of glorious and terrific sandhills . . . However I must not talk of the hills too much . . . there is plenty of fine, open rolling golf country, and it is a feature of many of the holes that the shot has not merely to be hit into the air but hit into the strategic place for the playing of the second. The golf is emphatically in the grand manner.'

Genesis of both the club and the course is said to be a group of undergraduates who in 1888 started playing on the turf around St Enodoc Church and by Daymer Bay; and the official creation of a club is believed to have been in 1891. But it was not until 1907 that the great golfer James Braid—victor of many tournaments—laid out a full eighteen hole course which was altered in part in the early 1920s.

Brenda Duxbury afloat on the Camel.

52

The tenancy, originally granted by Dr Hoskin in 1905, was renewed until 1949 when the Duchy of Cornwall, through the Secretary Sir Clive Burn, took over all the land and accepted the Club as tenants under a lease.

The main course is of championship standard; a nine-hole course was opened in 1967 and later extended to eighteen holes. They share the magnificent views over estuary and farmland, but the shorter course is more suitable for the beginner and high handicapper. Not least for the non-golfers, there is a very pleasant walk over the soft, springy turf, your route being guided by discreetly placed white stones.

St Enodoc has had its Royal connections. Back in 1921—the year that Southern Ireland became the Irish Free State of Eire—the Prince of Wales, the late Duke of Windsor, came to lunch at the club house, after which he accepted the Presidency of St Enodoc, a position he retained until succeeding to the throne. More recently, in 1950, there was a visit by Their Majesties King George VI and Queen Elizabeth who, with their daughter Princess Margaret, took tea with the Club Captain and the Committee.

ST ENODOC CHURCH

Situated under Brae Hill on the edge of the golf course is St Enodoc Church.

Here, standing by the churchyard, opposite the west face of the Atlantic, it is hard to appreciate that, once, Daymer Bay was a forest inhabited by wild animals. Moreover this is no pure-speculation, for in 1857 a fierce Atlantic gale moved the sands to such an extent stumps and roots of trees and the horns and teeth of animals were exposed. But before long the sands hid them again, and today we have to use our imagination.

St Enodoc Church, with its little spire pointing like a crooked finger into the sky, began life some seven hundred years ago. It has suffered badly at the hands of Nature. Early in the 1800s the adjoining commons were nothing more than shifting sands and the

St Enodoc Golf Club has one of the finest, most testing courses in the Westcountry.

church was so buried that, at one stage, in order to keep the tithes the parson and his loyal clerk had to be lowered through a skylight for the only service of the year!

The restoration of St Enodoc took place during 1863-64 and an interesting first-hand account dated 1919-21 still exists. It was in the handwriting of Mr Hart Smith Pearce, the son of the Reverend Hart Smith, who was responsible for restoring the chapel. '. . . the sands had blown higher than the eastern gable, the wet came in freely, the high pews were mouldy-green and worm-eaten and bats flew about, living in the belfry. The communion table had two short legs because the rock projected at the foot of the east wall. In 1864 the building was restored, the walls partly rebuilt and on good foundations, the sand removed and the little churchyard cleared and fenced with a good wall, and the roof renewed and new seats provided. It all cost about £650 and I remember the pains and energy my father spent to raise the money . . . These works were done by the masons and the workmen of the parish . . . with loving care and nothing was destroyed needlessly or removed if it was of use or interest.'

From the same hand-written account came an unusual story of the chalice. 'When my father was first inducted in 1851 he saw in one of the farmhouses, a beautiful Elizabethan chalice, and he felt certain it belonged to St Enodoc. He could never obtain possession but was put off with promises, and, of course, he could not prove his suspicions. He kept his eye on it year after year. After he left in 1871 he still kept the chalice under observation, until a new generation came. Visitors appeared frequently and the value of the plate being often discussed, all old pledges were forgotten and a stranger was allowed to purchase it. My father traced him but was again baffled. Finally he heard the chalice was to be sold at Christie's and by shrewd diplomacy and enlisting the sympathy of the firm and other friends, he secured it for £13.10s.0d. and restored it after fifty years to the St Enodoc Chapel. No doubt the farmer or his parents had originally, as churchwardens, had charge of the plate, and, being seldom used, thought it ornamental on the kitchen shelf.'

In Norman times the church was cruciform in shape with a tower to the north. The out-of-perpendicular spire is a thirteenth-century addition; and the doorway under the porch was added a century later. In the days of the first Elizabeth the church boasted two bells, but these were sold towards the end of the last century. The present

*St Enodoc Church—at one time buried in the shifting
sand dunes—now the burial place of Sir John Betjeman.*

bell was acquired in 1875—the year that General Booth founded the
Salvation Army and the first Barnado Home opened its doors—
from an Italian ship, the *Immacolata* wrecked on the rocks of
Greenaway, roughly halfway between Polzeath and Daymer Bay.
Strangely, though, the bell is inscribed *Sachel.* Did it perhaps
belong to an earlier ship?

Many recorded burials at St Enodoc are of 'unknown sailors', men
whose ships perished on the notorious Doom Bar. Some graves are
two and three tiers deep: grim reminders of Parson Hawker's warning words:

*From Hartland Point to Padstow Light
Is a watery grave by day and by night.*

This of course is the beloved church of Sir John Betjeman, the
most famous Poet Laureate of all times. He died peacefully in his

sleep, at 8 o'clock on Saturday morning 19 May 1984 not far away at Trebetherick. He was buried here in St Enodoc churchyard on Tuesday 22 May alongside the graves of unknown sailors whose ships had perished on the Doom Bar. It was a simple service—strictly private at the request of his family—the tiny church decorated with wild flowers; oil lamps and candles providing the only light. They carried his coffin between sand dunes in driving rain, almost gale force conditions—the kind of weather that might have triggered another poem.

They called him the People's Poet, but as Kenneth Young wrote in his obituary in *The Sunday Telegraph:* 'He was delighted to become Poet Laureate, though he was no snob; he just preferred dining with Dukes than with dustmen . . .' Sir John loved our wide Cornish skies, the beaches and the changing sea, the cliffs and the churches and, above all, treasured his boyhood memories of a vanished Cornish way of life. He fell in love with Cornwall as a child, and it was a love affair that never ended, for though he wrote movingly of other places, Cornwall called him again and again, firing his writing —like a first love that would not let go.

CHRIST AND THE CAMEL?

Did Christ—as a boy—sail up the Camel?

There is, in fact, a legend claiming that Jesus, with Joseph of Arimathea, came on a tin-collecting visit to Cornwall. The local version is that the boy came ashore at St Minver to get fresh water for the ship. The Jesus Well is marked by that name on the appropriate Ordnance Survey map. Standing in the middle of the golf course today, it still provides a water supply.

The Quiller Couches, on a visit in the 1890s, discovered that children suffering from whooping cough, were still taken to drink the waters . . .'pins were dropped in for the telling of fortunes and even money was cast into its depths for the same reason . . . one particular Sunday . . . as much as sixteen shillings were taken out by

Sir John Betjeman 'fell in love with Cornwall as a child, and it was a love affair that never ended . . .'

58

unbelievers who then reaped the benefit of the superstitions of others.'

Some places are not dumb. Assuming we have the humility and the patience to listen, they somehow manage to speak to us. Look, for instance, at Brea Hill with its ancient burial mounds silhouetted on the skyline. Here you are coming face to face with distant history. In 1822 an ancient oratory was discovered beneath it when another gale lifted huge quantities of sand. But, as with the forest, it has disappeared like a ghost. The discovery of Roman glass beads, Samian ware and coins—third and fourth century—might suggest a Roman settlement. Interestingly, found with them were a rude coral necklace and other articles. Some places set us questions; make us think. This is such a setting.

DAYMER BAY, TREBETHERICK

Daymer Bay is a beautiful inlet where the estuary broadens towards the Atlantic from Rock—you can walk all the way at low tide—and a pleasant walk it is. A crescent of sand, with shelter, Daymer Bay is an ideal spot for bathing. But here or anywhere else on this North Cornish coast, it is as well to remember that bathing fatalities occur every year.

Should you be at the wheel of a motor car, you can approach Daymer Bay via Trebetherick, taking the road by Trebetherick Post Office that winds its way down to a spacious car park on the low grassy cliff. Inevitably in the holiday season it is heavily populated. However, at low tide the beach stretches itself to the extent of comfortably accommodating an army.

Obviously if you can choose your dates in the year, avoid the high holiday season, unless you are looking for the gaiety of crowds, and that will be found in the bigger resorts like Newquay and St Ives. Those looking for a quieter holiday, or seeking the essential soul of Cornwall in comparative peace and quiet, should come early in May or June, or late in September or early October. Cornwall is probably at her best in spring when the hedgerows and woods are splashed with colour. Then nature is stirring. Scent is in the air, and the landscape almost becomes a kaleidoscope.

Sir John Betjeman nostalgically recalled his boyhood by the Camel. 'Trebetherick . . . it may have been a suburb by the sea and

*In 1944 the then Duchess of Kent spent a family
holiday at Trebetherick.*

for all our crabbing, fishing and bathing, nothing to do with the real
Cornish who regarded us as the foreigners we still are. But for me it
was home for the eyes, the nose and the ears. The great, black half-
moon of Bray Hill with its three cairns on the top, the long low
stretch from Padstow to Stepper Point on the other side of the
estuary. The regular cragginess of Newland's rocky island. The
changing vegetation on the high-hedged lane . . . all these for the
eyes. For the nose there was the scent of seaweed and salty sand.
Wild mint at one season, honeysuckle and thyme at the other; and
drying cow-dung always. For the ear there was the roar on the shore

61

when the tide was high. The utter silence when it was low. The larks and oyster-catchers shrill and small, and sea-gulls wailing like angry babies. The rumble of the London and South-Western as it crossed the viaduct on its way to the Padstow terminus, the end of that long, slow journey of the ambitiously named Atlantic Coast Express.'

POLZEATH

A curling cliff path leads you on to Greenaway, across the springy turf, past private houses that face only the Atlantic and the sky— some of the most expensive properties of their kind in Cornwall and on to one of North Cornwall's most popular resorts, Polzeath. Despite the multiplication of bungalows, cafes and car parks, it remains a superlative setting. Hayle Bay—a name curiously hardly mentioned—is a splendid surfing rendezvous. Here water, with the power of the Atlantic beyond it, comes thundering in; sometimes with the wind-whipped fury of a storm, and at other times a gentler rhythmic surge, as on say a hot, golden summer beach.

Surf, to the surfer, is Life with a capital L.

Perceptively one painter has portrayed surf in the form of white horses, for it literally kicks and bucks—and rears. Somebody has said that where you find the sea, you find surf, and where you find surf, you meet beauty.

Certainly here at Polzeath you can only agree.

Sabine Baring-Gould, squire and parson for so long at Lewtrenchard just beyond Launceston, and author of that famous hymn *Onward Christian Soldiers,* set his novel *In the Roar of the Sea* here at Polzeath on this North Cornish coast. It is a racy tale of dark nights and darker deeds: a mixture of wrecking and plunder. Its heroine is eighteen-year-old Judith Trevisa who desperately tried to protect her brother from evil influences. She alone dared to defy Captain Coppinger, the man they called Cruel Coppinger. There are many

62

better novels in the Cornish library, but we recommend it as a 'good read'. The story of Cruel Coppinger is thought to be based on fact but these unlawful activities probably took place further up the coast.

As you cross Polzeath beach and look around the bay to Pentire Point it is difficult to imagine that lead and silver were mined here for more than two centuries. Hamilton Jenkin, the Cornish mining historian, records the first mention of the lode in 1580 which he said can still be seen in the cliffs and the Pentire Mine was known to be working in the seventeenth century. In the 1850s under the grand title of the Pentire Glaze and Pentire United Silver-lead Mines, shafts were drained to a depth of two hundred feet by an adit cut to the sea. But little trace can be seen today of the engine house, steam whim, crusher and water wheel. The *West Briton* records how one Saturday night in 1819 a 'barge conveying lead ore raised from the mine at Pentire Glaze to Padstow, being on her passage from Trebetherick where the ore is shipped, was struck by a heavy sea and being heavily laden, instantly foundered. Of the nine men on board, six perished.'

The cliffs at Polzeath in 1956.

PENTIRE

To climb the path to Pentire Point is a must for every fit visitor. From the windswept top of this volcanic outcrop a world of its own spreads out below. You can look back up the estuary and down to Trevose, with its lighthouse. Rumps Point, the eastern flank of Pentire Head looks like a gigantic stegosaurus climbing out of the sea.

The ramparts across the narrow neck of this promontory stand out even more dramatically when seen silhouetted against the sky from sea. It's difficult to imagine the Iron Age builders of this cliff castle living permanently on such an inhospitable headland. Perhaps it was only used for protection when under attack. Yet recent excavations have shown several huts to have been built within the fortifications and large quantities of animal bones, limpet and mussel shells and pottery indicate considerable occupation. The ramparts were quite sizeable, the middle of the three being built of slate dug from the ditch in front of it and probably topped by a stone parapet and fronted with a revetment of boulders. Large postholes indicate a wooden gate at the entrance through the ramparts. Some wooden fragments were thought to belong to a loom which would certainly lead one to believe that the occupation was more than temporary.

From here you can see Tintagel Castle, on a fine day Hartland Point, and, on rare occasions when the light is just right, Lundy Island. Lundy Island, over forty miles away, incredibly seems to rise out of the sea almost within arm's reach.

Arthur Norway maintained that this magnificent stretch of cliffs from Pentire was 'beyond comparison the finest in all Cornwall'.

One day a poet, sitting on the cliffs somewhere here above Polzeath, found the beauty of the coastline stirring thoughts elsewhere.

Rumps Point—like a gigantic stegosaurus climbing out of the sea. Iron Age men built ramparts across the narrow neck.

Before long, a poem was beginning to take shape in the man's head. Its opening ran:

With proud thanksgiving, a mother for her children,
England mourns for her dead across the sea . . .

The poet was Laurence Binyon and the poem *For the Fallen* which, when published, captured the hearts of the British people, and ensured its author a kind of immortality. When the 1914-18 war was over, *For the Fallen* seemed a natural tribute for all who had perished in the conflict, and was adopted as such by the British Legion. Its famous fourth line—'They shall not grow old, as we that are left grow old'—is even today quoted on Remembrance Sunday. The poet, that day near Polzeath, was apparently thinking in particular of the Retreat from Mons.

THE OTHER SIDE OF THE CAMEL

Now let us explore the other flank of the estuary. The character upstream is so different from the wider estuary mouth at Rock. There is no easy access by road; therefore people are few and the

One of the flooded slate quarries opposite Cant Hill
with silent engine houses and waste heaps.

atmosphere quiet. Understandably it is a favourite spot for bird-watchers.

What better way to explore than by boat—ghosting under sail with the tide. You may be lucky and see a solitary heron or a flock of oyster-catchers taking off from the beach, their wings with the precision of a troupe of ballet dancers turning black to white.

Today, not even a train disturbs the peace, but stone arches under now-quiet railway embankments invite exploration of the streams that flow into the estuary. There are creeks and mudbanks and magical sounding names like Tregunna and Halwyn. The most important development in the life of the Camel in recent years has been the opening up of the old railway line as a footpath for walkers.

Opposite Cant Hill the character of the landscape changes again. There are the remains of landing stages where boats once moored to take off slate. This is a stark quarried landscape with heaps of waste slate and terraces, flooded quarries and silent engine houses. The slate here was grey with a purplish tinge and used for flagstones, chimney pieces, water tanks and roofing slates.

ST ISSEY AND LITTLE PETHERICK

In our earlier version, *Along The Camel,* we were taken to task by a proud resident of St Issey who considered his parish truly part of Camel Country. So this time, we include it.

One unimaginative travel writer has described the road from Wadebridge to Padstow as 'uninteresting'. How can you travel through places like St Issey and Little Petherick and use such a word? Our Cornish villages are packed with incident—and history.

Here at St Issey you will find a church so old that nobody, for certain, can date its consecration. A curiously underphotographed building we think because Ray's shot of it on a beautiful October afternoon is the first we have seen. North of the church town narrow lanes lead down to the Camel and Little Petherick creek. Here-abouts are some of the loveliest acres in the countryside of North Cornwall.

Looking down on Little Petherick: 'There is an aged wharf and quay'.

St Issey Church: 'Our Cornish villages are packed with incident—and history.'

South of St Issey, the landscape moved Sir John Betjeman to write: '. . . luxuriant and unspoiled inland Cornwall with villages of old cottages, like Trenance and Tredinnick, and the wooded valleys of moorland streams coming from St Columb Down.'

Little Petherick is a sheltered valley with an inlet, off the western bank of the estuary. There is an aged wharf and quay. Upstream, the landscape is wooded and miraculously unscarred. Hereabouts you can get an inkling of the Cornwall that once was: before the motor car came and tourism exploded. During the summer months, though, this narrow, twisting Wadebridge to Padstow road is busy with traffic. So much so that few people risk stopping and getting out of their cars. Where the road bridges a stream is the Church of St Petroc. It is a shrine of Anglo-Catholicism. A yew tree stands in the churchyard. The church has an arcade dating from the fifteenth century. Thanks to the generosity of the Molesworth family and Athelstan Riley, the church is filled with treasures. There are some magnificent old bench ends, and three volumes of *Fox's Book of Martyrs*—all chained. The screen is comparatively new, carved and painted in medieval tints, and has a loft and Crucifixion with two angels plus Mary and John. This was designed by Sir Ninian Comper who was also responsible for most of the other fittings, and

69

the beautiful glass of the east window. According to Sir John Betjeman the church was as good as rebuilt by William White in 1858 for the Tractarian rector, Sir Hugh Molesworth. In the Molesworth Chapel, in an old plaster panel are four figures, carved and painted. Here too you will find a beautiful lady, Andalusia, wife of the former Patron Athelstan Riley, who gave sixteenth and seventeenth-century vestments and plate, and designed the village hall in 1907. Andalusia died in 1912, and her bronze figure is on a grey slate tomb, her head and feet, resting on cushions. She is wearing a dress with embroidered borders to the sleeves and neck. 'The memory of her beautiful face,' thought Arthur Mee, the author, 'is the best thing the traveller takes away from here.'

Climbing out of Little Petherick on the same Padstow road, you will find a garden centre. Here part of the old road, now no more than a well-concealed lay-by, curling like a 'C' going in the right direction, is the site of several serious Supernatural claims. One man, who has seen something here beyond human explanation, is

Alan Sandry: 'That bit of road,' he recalled, 'was part of the old priest's path that stretched from Padstow to Bodmin. It was certainly a monk-like figure . . . I've got within ten or twelve paces of it, and have tried to converse with it; said I was a Christian and wanted to know if I could help. It was shrouded . . . grey robes . . . it was bright moonlight, and it appeared to be solid, but it didn't cast a shadow.'

If you're contemplating doing a spot of ghost-hunting of your own, you should know these claims have all been made late at night, and as early as 1.55 in the morning. Moreover it would seem that whenever anyone has tried to make conversation with this strange little figure, he or she has inexplicably vanished.

Just beyond the haunted lay-by, you will join the B3274. Away to your right is Dennis Hill, from where there are superlative views across the estuary and out to sea. The 56-foot monument commemorates the Jubilee of Queen Victoria.

Two views from Dennis Hill.   Left: looking up the estuary towards Wadebridge. The railway crosses Little Petherick Creek on its way to Padstow.   Below: the remains of the old tide mill in Little Petherick Creek.

Looking across the estuary to Padstow from Daymer Bay—a panorama of sea, sand and sky.

PADSTOW

The railway, of course, changed the face of Cornwall in that it brought the holidaymakers, and sowed the seeds of expanding tourism. The most concrete reminder of that in Padstow is the Metropole Hotel, originally named the South Western Hotel, built in 1900 by the Corys, a well-known shipping family. Now part of the Trust House Forte group, the Metropole boasts magnificent views over the great, sandy sweep of the Camel.

If you come to Padstow in winter—when the visitors have gone or their numbers have become only a trickle—you will come closest to catching the spirit of old Padstow—providing you forget the double yellow lines, the TV aerials and all the other bits and pieces that make up that rather frightening thing we call 'progress'. Now you can walk easily in these narrow streets. Some of the shops are shut, and the gulls make their presence felt in a way that only people, living within sight and sound of the sea, can appreciate and understand.

In these off-season months, the old buildings—not all pretty by any means—the crooked alleyways, twisting uphill, turning under aged archways, and giving into tiny, very private courtyards, all combine in giving us a glimmer of the Padstow that once was. Even on a grey day, Padstow, at this time, can be an experience as interesting as when the crowds choke it on May Day. Now the accent of the bar is essentially Cornish, and you begin to understand that the painter Peter Lanyon was right when he said: 'The Cornishman is fond of private secrets. A solemn intercourse of

Heather Griffiths captures the spirit of Padstow in the 1920s.

native with native, often intimate, is mistaken for a gossip . . . The bush telegraph which puts the GPO to shame is part of this intimate revelation from native to native.'

Between say November and March, the outsider coming inside Padstow will find the truth of those words.

If you stand on the 'Obby 'Oss slip when a strong westerly wind is blowing, you would hardly know it: a perfect setting for the harbour tucked around the corner from the open sea and sheltered from prevailing westerlies by a steep hill beyond.

Little wonder St Petroc chose this spot after his crossing from Wales some 1400 years ago. The stories and legends surrounding him are many. He came of a noble family in Wales, but did not wish to inherit his father's kingdom. Instead as a youth he went to Ireland to study under renowned Christian teachers. Inspired to spread the Gospel he sailed to Cornwall arriving in a boat not much bigger than a Welsh coracle. Perhaps he landed at Trebetherick, the place of Petroc, and there met the reapers, who taunted him to demonstrate his holiness. St Petroc is reputed to have struck the rock with his staff and immediately a fountain of the purest water flowed.

His monastery here at Padstow became an important religious centre. Later he founded the Bodmin community—the Priory surviving until the Reformation.

In the turbulent years before the Norman Conquest, the coasts of Britain suffered greatly from Viking raids and Cornwall was no exception. The monastery at Padstow was destroyed by the Vikings in 981; its valuables made it a ready target. The *Anglo Saxon Chronicle* records the disaster:

'In this year S Petroc's stowe was sacked and the same year very great damage was done everywhere by the coast in Devon and Cornwall.' The monastery almost certainly ended in flames and the monks removed to Bodmin.

It is this event that Anya Seton, the historical novelist, has chosen as central to her novel *Avalon*, set in the last quarter of the tenth century: a period of conflict between Church and State, and the threat of Viking invaders. It is a vivid, fast-moving piece of

Michael Williams with Margaret Rowe in the Strand
Bookshop in Padstow—'filled from floor to ceiling . . .'

fiction with enough historical research to give us a glimpse of North Cornwall nearly a thousand years ago.

We, at Bossiney, have a special affection for the Strand Bookshop at Padstow. Not only does it embody all those qualities of the old-fashioned bookshop, it was one of our very first customers when we launched into publishing back in the 1970s—and it has gone on giving us first-class support ever since.

In 1986 the bookshop acquired a kind of literary fame. You will find it inside the pages of a romantic novel, entitled *Impulsive Challenge* written by Margaret Mayo, and published by Mills and Boon.

Gisele, the central character in the novel, visits Padstow:

'. . . Another hour was spent in a bookshop on the Strand. It was filled from floor to ceiling in glorious disarray. As well as new books and paperbacks there were secondhand and antiquarian books on almost every subject under the sun. Books about Cornwall, maps, prints. It was a fascinating shop and Gisele could have stayed there all day, except that she was afraid Catherine might worry if she did not return soon.'

The Church of St Petroc at Padstow stands high above the town surrounded by grey headstones.

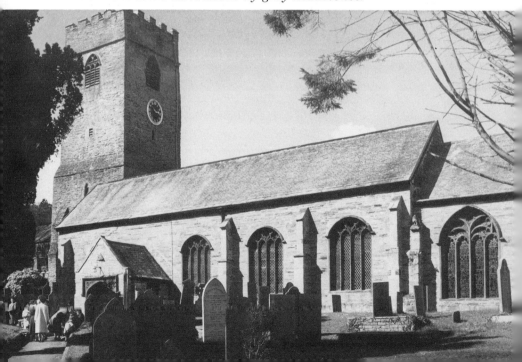

So St Petroc gave his name to the town—Petroc's Stowe, but Padstow has had many names. Among these was Adelstowe, meaning old place or town, or it could owe something to King Athelstan who probably granted Padstow the special privilege of sanctuary. Thieves and felons escaped the law by remaining within the immediate area of the church often giving the town a bad reputation, but the Reformation changed all that.

The exact site of St Petroc's monastery is debatable. Some say it is where the church stands now. Others believe it was higher up at Prideaux Place where St Samson, yet another Cornish saint, lived as a hermit. But the large shaft and base of a cross near the south east gate of the churchyard, found when digging a grave, perhaps indicates the church and monastery were both here.

The present Church of St Petroc stands high above the town, set in a gentle green hollow framed by trees, and surrounded by grey headstones. It is mainly fifteenth century, though the base of the tower is two centuries earlier. In the porch you'll find eight-holed wooden stocks and you perhaps begin feeling sorry about the insults and abuse that must have been physically and verbally hurled at the men and women locked to them.

Inside the church, there is plenty to see. Especially beautiful is the finely carved fifteenth-century font bearing figures of the twelve Apostles; it is made of a dark catacleuse stone from the cliffs hard by Harlyn Bay. Tradition has it that anyone baptised in it would be preserved from the gallows. Alas the magic failed to work for a man named Elliott who had been christened there, as he was hanged about 1800 for robbing the mail.

On the steps of the sanctuary is the engraved brass of Laurence Merther who was vicar here in the 1400s. Against the south aisle wall is an imposing monument to the Prideaux family: the kneeling figures of Sir Nicholas Prideaux (dated 1627), his wife and four sons; father in armour and sons in long capes and ruffs. The monument also remembers William Morice, who married Sir Nicholas's grand-daughter; knighted when Charles II landed at Dover, he was made Secretary of State for his services in the Restoration.

There is some fine stained glass. You can see King Edmund with arrows, Michael with burning sword, and Nicholas with a vessel. There are also three women saints with scenes from their careers: Catherine discussing—probably disagreeing—with doctors, Winifred sewing, and Cecilia with her husband and an angel. Not

77

forgetting St Petroc himself in the modern east window carrying his Abbot's crozier.

Until 1538 the Prior of Bodmin was Lord of the Manor of Padstow, the last being Prior Vivian, whose tomb lies in the sanctuary of Bodmin Parish Church. It was during the sixteenth century at the time of the Reformation when Henry VIII confiscated the great estates of the monasteries, that the lands of St Petroc's original monastery came into the possession of the Prideaux family, and Sir Nicholas instructed builders to start work on the mansion that became Prideaux Place. Soon it was a place of importance in the county with the Prideaux family playing a major role in the affairs of Cornwall. It was seemingly little troubled during the Civil War. The family were staunch Royalists, and there is a theory that the King was sheltered at Prideaux Place, following the Parliamentarians' crushing victory at Naseby.

Probably the most famous of the family was Humphry Prideaux. Educated at Westminster School, he was elected to Christ Church, Oxford, and became a highly respected scholar. In 1702 he was appointed Dean of Norwich, and despite serious illness—he underwent major surgery long before the invention of anaesthetics *and* the surgeon botched the job—he made valuable contributions to theological research. He died in 1724 and his tomb appropriately is inside Norwich Cathedral.

With embattled and creepered walls, projecting bays and mullioned windows, Prideaux Place remains today Padstow's most imposing residence. Trees and parkland are rare sights in North Cornwall but here at Padstow a half circle of trees protects the manor, the church and the former borough of Padstow from the prevailing westerlies. The house is only open to the public on special occasions but you can obtain a good view from the road to Tregirls, and if you're lucky you will actually see deer in the park. This, of course, is one of the few manor houses in the county still lived in by the family who built it. There is an interesting legend to the effect that when the deer leave Prideaux Place, the Prideaux-Brune family will leave it too. The whole area owes a debt to the family who have done so much for preservation.

Inside the house, there is some fine carving by Grinling Gibbons, a fireplace and staircase from the Grenville's home at Stowe, and some pictures by John Opie, Cornwall's most celebrated portrait painter. When only a boy, dressed in a plain jacket, Opie, the son of a carpenter at St Agnes, arrived at the house one morning and proceeded to paint the entire family, including the pet dogs. Later Opie returned home, dressed in a handsome coat, lace ruffles and silk stockings, gleefully producing twenty guineas and predicting that, in future, he would support himself. It was no idle boast, for though Opie's career was to have its troughs, his finest work won golden opinions, Sir Joshua Reynolds once saying, 'This youth begins where most artists leave off . . .'

It was Queen Elizabeth I who granted Padstow borough status but the Prideaux family objected fearing a reduction in their power, and Padstow corporation subsequently disappeared. But not before one Ann Calwoodly caused a scene in the church. A new pew had been installed for the mayor and the lady reacted vehemently to the extent of bringing an axe to church to smash the pew to pieces. We learn that she was brought before the Court of Star Chamber, but we do not know her fate.

An Edwardian party at Prideaux Place—still lived in by the family who built it.

THE HARBOUR

Padstow was, of course, the haunt of great Westcountry seadogs. Sir John Hawkins, for example, in 1565 found shelter here from the autumn gales on his return from the West Indies. Later Sir Martin Frobisher, returning from his quest for the North West Passage to China, was also relieved to find shelter here. Sir Walter Raleigh came too.

On the south quay, hard by the Old Customs House Inn, you will find his Court House. Standing behind spiked railings, it overlooks the modern harbour office and car park. Raleigh, explorer, sailor, poet and courtier—one of the most colourful figures of the Elizabethan age—came from Budleigh Salterton down on the South

Devon coast, but in his role as Warden of the Stannaries of Cornwall, he held his Court here and collected legal dues. In our mind's eye, we can try to picture the immaculately dressed man with dark curling hair arrogantly striding through these narrow streets. The Queen showered favours upon him, including responsibility for the rich Cornish tin mines.

Another ancient building that encourages us to look back into history is Abbey House, standing on the North Quay, from which a subterranean passage was constructed, linking it some say with the ill-fated monastery. It is thought to have been a one-time Guild House of the Padstow merchants.

The history of Padstow has always had a seafaring flavour, whether trading or fishing or shipbuilding. This Guild of St Petroc was formed by the traders of the town to finance joint stock fishing ventures.

Left: Abbey House on North Quay, Padstow, some say linked by an underground passage to the monastery. Below: Padstow harbour today.

Looking across the estuary from Padstow to the sand dunes at Ferry Point, Rock.

The whole of medieval Padstow—including the harbour—belonged to the Priory at Bodmin, so harbour tithes were paid to the Abbot. Prideaux Place was built on the site of the monks' tithe barn. In Chaucer's day, Padstow was on the route for the medieval pilgrims travelling to Rome from Ireland and Wales. They would land at Padstow and thence journey by land to Fowey or St Michael's Mount for re-embarkation for the Continent or directly by sea to the Mediterranean. There were many Irish people in Padstow in medieval times: the direct result of these trading connections across the Irish Sea. Coasting vessels also traded up the Bristol Channel and across to Brittany.

In 1540, the King's Librarian, John Leland came to Cornwall when researching his survey of England. His notes recorded that many small Breton ships tied up at the Padstow quays exchanging goods from France for Padstow fish. He described it as 'a good quik fisschar toun but onclenly kepte'.

In the seventeenth and eighteenth centuries trade increased with the expansion of mining—copper, antimony and lead ores being included with other exports of grain, cured fish and slate. The port handled imports from Ireland of glass and linen, salted pork and tallow; linen and canvas came from Brittany and salt, wine and vinegar also from France; malt and hardware from the Severn ports. But it was in the nineteenth century that the main expansion took place. Timber was then brought from Scandinavia and from as far as Canada. These same ships, on their outward journeys, took to the New World those emigrants from the Old, victims of the agricultural and mining slumps of the nineteenth century.

In her heyday Padstow harbour must have been a wonderful sight—the quays packed and larger vessels moored in the Pool, the deep water anchorage beyond: brigs and brigantines, smacks and schooners, barquentines and square riggers. Padstow naturally then boasted several shipbuilding yards. In the Padstow Museum, housed in the Institute over the Library, Bill Lindsey showed us tools he had preserved from Brabyn's Yard, or Lower Yard. You can almost hear the ring of the adze as the timbers were shaped and smell the Stockholm tar as the seams were payed with pitch after caulking the joints with oakum. An old photograph shows the building of the last pilot cutter. Pilot gigs, slightly built, went out in all weather, often staying at sea in order to be the first aboard any approaching vessel to bring her safely to harbour. Before the first lifeboats, it was often these pilot gigs that went to the help of vessels in danger.

The advent of iron and steam ships killed boatbuilding in Padstow, but the beginning of this century saw a revival in the fishing industry, not only among local boats. The East coast drifters made Padstow their centre for winter fishing of the 'Klondike', the name given to the rich fishing grounds off the North Cornish coast. With the coming of the railway fish could be sent direct to London. This, too, was the era of the ice factory on the quay.

One well-known and much-loved Camel character was Bill Orchard who spent a lifetime fishing out of the estuary.

'One day up off Hartland,' he recalled, 'we came up to our marker buoy which was bobbing about more than usual . . . and what did we find? A shark, a porbeagle it was, caught in a load of cotton waste tangled round the staff.'

Bill started work at the age of eleven during the First World War on one of the Lowestoft sailing trawlers fishing off Padstow. They operated between Padstow and Swansea where they would land fish and take on ice and coal for they had a small donkey engine to work the capstan for heaving the trawl. But being wartime, there were extra hazards for fishermen. Bill told the story how . . . 'One day thirteen trawlers sailed out of the estuary, but only thirteen dinghies rowed back in. It was a German submarine put paid to that day's fishing off Newland Island at the mouth of the river. At least the fishermen were allowed to take to their dinghies before their boats were sunk.'

On a lighter note Bill, before his death, told of the day they were becalmed off Lundy Island and fishing had come to a halt. Here they were approached by a Naval boat patrolling the Bristol Channel.

'Any fish on board?'

'No wind—no fish!'

'Tell you what, if we give you a tow so that you can shoot your trawl, we'll go halves on the catch.'

And so it was. The Navy provided the day's power and both crews supped well that night.

Superstition and the sea have long been close relations. And Padstow fishermen were no exceptions. A *West Briton* report, published in December 1848, said: 'Within the last few weeks, the fishing boats of Padstow have caught several thousands of herrings, but one boat being more unfortunate than the others, some persons persuaded the crew that the boat was bewitched. They then determined to break the charm by nailing a horseshoe to the bottom of the boat, which they did, and the next night caught 1,400 fish, which confirmed the belief that the boat had been bewitched!'

In season here from Padstow you can take some interesting sea trips, some stretching as far north as Boscastle or south to Newquay. Many would say that this is the best, most romantic way of seeing Cornwall. Author Denys Val Baker, writing of the county seen from the sea in *My Cornwall*, enticed his readers with these words: 'The sun shines, the sea sparkles, the boat glides gently along on yet another fascinating pilgrimage, along one of the most intricate, the most mysterious, and the most beautiful coastlines in the whole wide world.'

That, of course, is the sunny face of the sea. But even Denys Val Baker admits there are stormy days when it is neither romantic nor

Bill Orchard who spent a lifetime fishing out of the estuary—a much-loved Camel personality.

84

mysterious and 'one would give almost anything in the world to be a thousand miles away from the cursed Cornish coastline!'

MAY DAY

Padstow, of course, has a special place in the fields of folklore on the strength of its 'Obby 'Oss festivities every May Day, when crowds and age-old customs turn the narrow streets into a cauldron of activity. Music, singing and dancing, excited crowds, eating and drinking all mingle with tradition, as do Padstonians and outsiders.

The Hobby Horse—or 'Obby 'Oss to the true Cornish—is a fearsome animal wearing a fierce mask, making him resemble a heathen god rather than a living horse. In front of the horse dances a local man carrying a club—he is called 'the teazer'. One spectator observed: 'The whole thing is grotesque, but is one of the most genuine folk customs surviving . . .'

The 'Obby 'Oss is, in fact, a man encased in a cloth mask, grimly black, save for the various coloured stripes on his cap and mask. He wears a tall cap with a flowing plume and tail and savage-looking wooden snappers. The cap, plume, tail and decoration of the snappers are all made of genuine horsehair. Jaws of the snappers are studded on the inside to multiply the noise, and these are operated by a string held by the man inside the 'Oss.

The Cornish historian, Thurstan Peter, thought this ceremony and the Helston Furry Dance to be 'pagan festivals of revival and fruitfulness and one of those forms of magic, not by any means implying the notion of invariable cause and effect, but an attempt to express in ritual the emotions and desires—and so to this have been grafted on the one-hand folklore, and on the other Christian ceremonies, the history being still further confused by mistaken efforts of well-meaning persons to remove elements regarded by them as coarse.'

Perhaps though it needs an outsider to set the scene vividly. Raymond Gardner, visiting the town for *The Guardian* in 1975 did just that with these words on the morning of the great day:

'And now Padstow sleeps fitfully in expectation of the summer rite to come. Walk quietly through the streets and you will hear, from behind the occasional lit window, the first strains of another song. It is the last practice. Then the children emerge in the lost shadows of the sunrise. Down through the twisting alleys, out through the arches, and into the public courtyards they come, in their garlands of flowers. Some carry branches of May, each is dressed in white and sports the red or blue sashes of the 'oss they will follow. By 7 a.m. the two children's 'Osses and the young Mayers are outside the Metropole Hotel and the well-heeled tourists are quickened from sleep by the persistent humming of the drums and the shrill call of the accordion.

'This is a preliminary. At 10 a.m. the crowd meets before the Institute. The Mayers have assembled—the men with their accordions, melodions, tambourines, and drums are poised for the song, the master of ceremonies struts about in top hat and tails, the

May Day 1897—the 'Obby 'Oss whirls like a dervish with his great hooped skirt.

The Teazer and 'Oss take a rest on May Day 1949—
the ceremony is an important part of Cornwall's
heritage.

Teazer appears with his clubs. Suddenly the Blue Ribbon 'Oss is upon us, whirling like a dervish, rearing against the crowd, his great hooped skirt lashing as he abandons himself to the dance and the Teazer's twitching hands. Stand back and let the beast have his moment. Stand firm and you may spend the remainder of your holiday gazing from the windows of the cottage hospital where they do a nice line in mending split skulls.'

One man, who knew May Day from the inside for many years, was David Farquhar, a former Rock-Padstow ferryman, later a book-seller on the Strand here at Padstow. An old advertisement announcing the 'Obby 'Oss ceremonies, states: 'led by our Dave'. 'That's me,' David Farquhar told us in 1976, 'I started carrying the 'Oss when I was only fifteen, and, in all, carried it for 25 years. When I started the 'Oss was weighing around 200 pounds. Back in

1943 I carried it all day. Normally you carry the 'Oss in bursts of about twenty minutes to half-an-hour. I certainly knew all about it that year . . . why next day I had to go to the doctor to have my shoulder stitched . . . had to have six or seven stitches where the shoulder straps had bitten into the flesh.'

His mother, who was born at nearby Hawker's Cove, was accordionist on the great day, incredibly until she was eighty-one; while his father, a Scot and seaman, also contributed to the occasion. In Padstow Museum you can see a splendid Blue Ribbon 'Obby 'Oss cap, made by Mr Farquhar Senior, which was used from 1946 until 1968.

The horse, of course, is a fertility symbol. And within the context of Padstow's May Day, a woman who is 'caught' by the 'Oss, trapped in under its skirts will, according to tradition, become 'lucky' or pregnant. Older residents recall unmarried women running down the streets to avoid 'capture'. But today's women accept 'the trapping' as a matter of sport.

Arise up Miss Smith and strew all your flowers
For summer is acome unto day
It is but a while ago since we have strewed ours,
In the merry morning of May.

At that, the dirge commences, the prancing 'Oss seemingly gives in before the Teazer's clubs. The cavortings halt as the animal goes down to the ground. The Teazer has baited the 'Oss and the club makes contact with the canvas.

O where is St George
O, where is he O?
He is out in his longboat on the salt sea O
Up flies the kite and down falls the lark O
Aunt Ursula Birdhood she had an old ewe
And she died in her own park O

Those lines indicate the length of legend and time contained in the May Day Song. Somehow St George seems to have got confused with St Petroc who is reputed to have rid Cornwall of its last dragon by luring it into the sea nearby.

*Looking towards Stepper across the Doom
Bar—many vessels have been wrecked here.*

Powerful publicity through the media now brings vast crowds to
Padstow for the ceremonies which makes life rather difficult for the
performing Padstonians; the singers for example, have problems in
following the leader's words above the noise and the bustle. But all,
who care for Cornwall's heritage, will hope that the people of
Padstow continue keeping their May Day full of zest and fun.

DOOM BAR

There are many legends surrounding the Doom Bar—that great,
grim, sandbank across the mouth of the estuary. The most common
is that a fisherman shot a mermaid with his arrow and in revenge

she cursed the harbour by placing this sandbar across the entrance. Legend got further confused when its formation was attributed to one Jan Tregeagle—a real live character much hated in the district for his ruthlessness. On his death, the story goes, he had to undertake various impossible tasks as penance to save his soul from the Devil. One was to drain Dozmary Pool on Bodmin Moor with a leaking limpet shell—another to plait a rope of sand and his many fruitless attempts resulted in the sandbar at the mouth of the estuary. There are many versions of this tale, but Arthur Norway tells us that he was of the Tregeagle family from the Parish of St Breock where you can see memorials to other members of his family in the church. There is no memorial to this famous 'Jan' Tregeagle and the pages in the Parish Registers which should have borne his signature have been removed.

The truth of Doom Bar, however, is even more dramatic than the fiction. It may provide shelter from the Atlantic swell for today's dinghy sailor, but it is a mixed blessing. Indeed, it has been the doom of many a vessel—appropriately named for probably more boats have been wrecked here than in any other comparable area. In his book *Cornish Shipwrecks*, Clive Carter puts the figure at 300 boats in 150 years.

The north coast of Cornwall is incredibly inhospitable, there being no other harbour of any size from Hartland to St Ives, apart from Newquay and neither of these offer a haven in a northerly gale or at low tide. Consequently vessels caught out in foul weather have often tried to gain the refuge of the Camel—only to be driven on to the Doom Bar.

In 1829 the Padstow Harbour Association for the Preservation of Life and Property from Shipwreck was formed. This was a unique move in the county: a scheme for assisting sailing vessels entering the narrow channel through the bar at Stepper Point. Once in the lee of the Point, they often found themselves becalmed under Stepper, and 'back-winded' by eddies. Three capstans were therefore sited near the Point. When the vessel was close in, the pilot boat would pass warps aboard from the capstans, enabling the craft to be winched through the narrow channel. At that time—and until the 1920s—the deep water channel, through Doom Bar, was on this, the Padstow side. Today though, the situation is reversed, with boats coming in close under Trebetherick Point, passing Gun Buoy which marks the deep channel.

*Launching the 'Arab' lifeboat at Hawker's Cove
which can be seen (right) looking seaward with a few
cottages and coastguard houses.*

The Association had the ambitious plan of blasting out a section of Stepper Point itself in order that sailing ships when rounding the headland might hold the 'true' wind. The plan of the scheme which we saw in the Padstow Museum shows you the amount of rock they intended to move, but although the excavation was started, it was never completed. Later quarrying finished the job. The Daymark on Stepper Point was erected at this time. Remember, it was several years before Trevose Lighthouse was built.

The 1820s also saw the first lifeboats, one supplied at Stepper in connection with this scheme and the other paid for by the people of Padstow, with the Lifeboat Institution contributing £10.

First sited in Padstow, the lifeboat was later stationed at Hawker's Cove nearer ships in distress. No effort was too much in those days for they would even transport the lifeboats on carriages to launch at the beach closest to the vessel in danger. This meant a shorter distance to row. The Lifeboat Station can still be seen at Hawker's Cove, although many will remember in more recent times, the *Joseph Hiram Chadwick* anchored in the Pool off Padstow, in order that she might always be afloat. The increased silting up of the Bar stopped her getting out easily at low water; so, at an estimated cost of £114,600 a new Lifeboat Station was built on the east side of Trevose Head in the open sea. Here the Duke of Kent in 1968 unveiled a commemorative plaque.

'From the cliff platform the Duke admired the impressive views of the North Cornwall coast,' wrote a *Cornish Guardian* reporter. 'Because of the strict timetable he was advised not to go down to the station, and after looking at the hundred or so concrete steps he would have to descend and ascend, he added jocularly:

'Perhaps it is just as well, after lunch!'

Here the new lifeboat can be launched swiftly at any state of tide in a bay protected from the prevailing wind and swell by the Merope

The Duchess of Kent chats with the lifeboat crew at Padstow in 1952 when she launched the new boat.

Rocks. It is a dramatic sight to see the lifeboat travel down a 240 foot slipway to join the Atlantic.

Earlier on that same day in 1968 the Duke, deputising for his mother Princess Marina who had gone into hospital, named at Padstow the new lifeboat *James and Catherine MacFarlane*. '. . . it was a split-second affair,' observed the same *Guardian* journalist, the lowest tide of the year 'gave the large lifeboat only a few inches of clearance under her keel as she rocked gently in the inner harbour.'

In 1984 Padstow received a new lifeboat, the *James Burrough*. She is 47 feet in length and the third of the very up-to-date Tyne class boats, with steel hull, aluminium superstructure, and seven watertight compartments all of which make her inherently self-righting. With a speed of 18 knots, twice as fast as the *James and Catherine Macfarlane*, she has an effective range of 250 miles offshore. This speed is possible because the Tyne class lifeboats have a flat transom and are fitted with trim tabs enabling the boat to lift almost on to the plane rather than having to throttle back in heavy seas. The crew of seven have to be strapped in as she is a very lively potent boat. Complete with the latest communications technology, she has achieved seventeen rescues in fourteen months. In April 1986 on a pitch black night she went to the help of a yacht *Seagoe* twelve miles offshore which was taking in water. A tow was secured. Her master stated that the crew would remain on board insisting that they were going to be all right. Within five minutes she sank, the lifeboat crew having to quickly cut the tow. Coxswain Trevor England, who holds two RNLI silver decorations for bravery, manoeuvred the boat to pick up within six minutes all four cadets, the master and the owner without hitting anyone in the water. Even in that short time the sailing master became too cold to grab the line and one of the lifeboat crew had to jump into the sea and grab him. Six lives were saved that night due to superb seamanship and teamwork, adding to the reputation of Padstow lifeboat, which, over the years, has affected some incredibly brave rescues.

Disaster though has struck twice. The first time was in 1867, when the second *Albert Edward* was called out to rescue the crew of a schooner which had been driven on to the Doom Bar. With gigantic waves running astern, she was swept along towards the schooner, when her drogue—the big canvas cone astern, employed to prevent 'somersaulting'—suddenly tore away. An enormous wave caught the boat aft and hurled her forward and over. All thirteen members of the lifeboat crew were thrown into the raging surf. Eight of them, exhausted yet alive, made the shore. But the bodies of the five others were later found on the rocks and in the dark gullies of Hell Bay, perhaps a more appropriate name for Hayle Bay.

One, who perished that day, was a man of remarkable courage. He was Daniel Shea, Chief Officer of Coastguards, who on retiring as coxswain on his promotion to Chief Officer, had continued to serve as a volunteer. Richard Tyacke, the then vicar of Padstow, referred to 'the brave Mr Shea', who had served two Padstow lifeboats and had helped in 'the saving of 45 lives'. A giant of a man—he was over

six feet tall—Daniel Shea won the RNLI silver medal and three other distinctions for gallantry in life-saving, including a medal especially struck by the Emperor of France for his heroic skill in rescuing the crew of a French ship wrecked near Padstow. He was only 42 when he died and was described by a journalist as 'almost a legendary figure not only in North Cornwall, but in the England of mid-Victorian times'.

The other Padstow disaster took place on the fateful night of 11 April 1900. This time, eleven men were lost including eight lifeboat men, and one trawler and two lifeboats were wrecked. One of these was the new *James Stephens* the first steam lifeboat which had been in service for just over a year. The trawler *Peace and Plenty* had dragged her anchor under Stepper during a vicious gale. She blew across the estuary in a maelstrom of surf grounding on Greenaway rocks where the Trebetherick rocket brigade managed to save all but three of her crew. Meanwhile the alarm had been raised on the Padstow shore and the old lifeboat, the *Arab*, was rowed through the surf to the other side of the estuary using a back channel round the bar. They searched in vain in the dark, and losing all but three oars, the boat too ended on Greenaway rocks, the crew scrambling to safety. Meanwhile, in answer to their flares, the *James Stephens* steamed out to Stepper and once clear of the Bar turned towards Polzeath. There she was hit by a gigantic sea on her quarter that knocked her broadside to the waves. She capsized with all but three of her crew drowned.

There was nearly a third disaster in 1944 when Bill Orchard, mentioned earlier, won the silver medal for gallantry and the award for the bravest lifeboat man of the year. It was on 23 November that the *Princess Mary* was called out. She was the largest lifeboat in service, and as her coxswain and second coxswain were newly appointed, it was Bill who took the helm. It took them only three hours to reach Knap Head near the Devon and Cornwall border where the Norwegian vessel, *Sjofna*, was on the rocks. She was carrying a cargo of china clay from Fowey to Larne in Ireland. The Clovelly lifeboat was already standing by but could not approach her as she was lying inside the breakers under the high cliffs. Large

Bill Orchard in 1945 with his silver medal awarded for gallantry—the bravest lifeboatman of the year.

waves were breaking over her and the crew were huddled on the bridge. 'Somebody just had to do something,' said Bill. 'The men on the top of the cliff had been trying to fire a line to the boat but without success.'

The dramatic story unfolded as the quiet Cornish voice continued.

With the coming of dawn, Bill anchored the lifeboat to seaward, then veered warp gradually so as to drift stern first towards the wreck. Heavy seas broke on their bows injuring one of the lifeboat crew. Bill had to give full power as each wave struck the boat in order to take the strain off the warp, thus enabling the anchor to hold.

Two lines were fired over the wreck but the crew were unable to make them fast, so Bill reanchored in a new position closer to the *Sjofna*. This brought the lifeboat into even shallower water. Two more lines were fired as the lifeboat struck bottom in the troughs. But this time the line was secured and a breeches buoy rigged, seven of the *Sjofna's* crew being brought to safety across the surf before the line chafed through.

As the tide dropped so the Hartland Life-Saving Apparatus Company managed after sixteen hours of trying, to get a line aboard. In the process the Captain had his leg broken by one of the rockets but eventually the rest of the crew were hoisted to safety up the cliff.

WRECKING AND SMUGGLING

This stretch of the Cornish coast was notorious for smuggling, and St Minver and St Merryn, in that order, were rated the top 'placing' districts in North Cornwall. One wreck at Polzeath had a cargo of sugar and rum. Something like a hundred casks of rum crashed against the rocks, and the spirits mingled with salt water in the hollows. Apparently there was much drunkenness. So much so that a man, named William Ham from Carvath, St Austell, who was working at Wadebridge at the time, drank so much that a local doctor was called. He employed a stomach pump, but without success.

A noted local wrecker was George Lee from St Merryn parish. He always carried a sword-stick. In his younger days he had served in the Navy and he thought nothing of walking fifty odd miles through the night from Plymouth to his home here on the North Cornish coast. At one stage in his smuggling career, Lee worked in partnership with a man called George Northcott. The pair found a quantity of gold coins on a wrecked ship by Bedruthan Steps. The cliffs there are nearly four hundred feet high—and there was only one path leading up from the beach. This route was blocked by a Crown officer, and Lee suggested the two men should separate, that Lee should take all the coins and travel across country; while Northcott should go straight home, and wait for Lee to come before they shared the spoils. Northcott eventually made home, but waited many hours before Lee turned up. Clothes covered in mud, Lee explained that he had been attacked and robbed of all the coins. Northcott believed him, but strange to relate it was not long after that Lee had enough money to buy a cottage and adjoining meadow.

Lee had the reputation of being afraid of nothing, but in his later years he lost his reputation when doing some carpentry for the farmer at Lower Trevorgus. Something of a handy man, Lee had gone there to repair the waterwheel. He was climbing up one side of the wheel when in his own words, he 'met myself coming down'. No amount of reasoning, by others, could convince him that he had not met himself coming down. As a result, he became more or less unbalanced.

Mother Ivey's Bay just east of Trevose Head was not always known as such. Times were when it was Polventon. But Mother Ivey, a dominant widow who farmed at Trevone, and whose land ran down to the bay, insisted that she had sole rights to all wreckage in the bay. She must have been a forceful lady, for nobody disagreed— at least to the extent of publicly disobeying her command. So much so that Polventon became known, to all, as Mother Ivey's Bay.

PADSTOW TO STEPPER

A favourite walk from Padstow takes you along the low cliffs to chapel stile on St Saviour's Point. Here near the site of St Saviour's chapel and the present-day war memorial, is a vantage point for watching the comings and goings of the estuary. Out to sea any boat rounding Stepper or Pentire is immediately visible and back towards Padstow you look down on the swimming pool, made out of rocks, and Ship-my-Pumps Point. One explanation of the name is that boats would not start pumping out the bilges until well clear of the harbour; another that it is a corruption of Chidley Pumps—small blowholes in the rocks.

A short walk seawards brings you to St George's Cove, a small bay with a varied history: not only the site of St George's holy well, there was once a brick-making kiln here and a quarry. St George's Cove was also a favourite picnic place for the gentry, the Prideaux-Brunes having a bathing hut here.

The coast sweeps round Tregirls sandy beach to Hawker's Cove, where there was once a chapel to St Samson. You can still see the old lifeboat houses and slipways and the coastguard houses in line up the hill. It is not many years since one of the locals would set off each evening at dusk from Hawker's to light the oil lamp on Stepper Point. During the First World War the Royal Flying Corps flew from Crugmeer just over the hill and they had six motor launches at

Stepper Point glimpsed through the tamarisk trees at Daymer Bay.

'... *these cliffs are ageless, unchangeable. They have withstood the sea. They will never be tamed.*'

Hawker's Cove to go out after enemy submarines. And in World War II the Fleet Air Arm flew from St Merryn, HMS *Curlew*, whose runways were built with stone from Stepper quarry.

The path to Stepper takes you above the site of this quarry. Roadstone was quarried and broken up by machinery on the site. It could be shot directly into lighters tied up at the pier in the deep water channel under Stepper. Within recent years all the rusting machinery has been dismantled and taken away for scrap, but the modified contours of Stepper remain visible to this day.

From the Coastguard hut on the top of the headland, you look out past the Daymark, along one of the finest cliff scenes in the county.

The very names excite you: Tregudda Gorge, Stack Rock, Marble Cliffs, the Cat's Back. Home of shags and cormorants, black-backed gulls and kittiwakes, the cliffs offer a challenge. Cornwall's attraction has been in her remoteness, the wild beauty of her cliffs, and loneliness of her moorland. Much of Cornwall is now tamed, but these cliffs are ageless, unchangeable. They have withstood the sea. They will never be tamed.

★ ★ ★

For us this has been a return to the Camel after nearly a decade. Of course there have been changes but there is still a remarkable sense of continuity about the river. Large stretches, we feel, have a strong renewing, recharging quality.

We thought of Ronald Duncan at the beginning of this journey and as we come to the edge of the Atlantic, we return to the poet. He thought that on a moor you 'cannot escape the feeling of the essential inhumanity, the being out of one's element: it is just as if one was at sea. It is in a valley through which a river flows that human values seem most important.'

ALSO AVAILABLE

NORTH CORNWALL IN THE OLD DAYS
by Joan Rendell, 147 old photographs
These pictures and Joan Rendell's perceptive text combine to give us many facets of a nostalgic way of North Cornish life, stretching from Newquay to the Cornwall/Devon border.
'This remarkable collection of pictures is a testimony to a people, a brave and uncomplaining race.' Pamela Leeds, The Western Evening Herald

COASTLINE OF CORNWALL
by Ken Duxbury
Ken Duxbury has spent thirty years sailing the seas of Cornwall, walking its clifftops, exploring its caves and beaches, using its harbours and creeks.
'... a trip in words and pictures from Hawker's Morwenstow in the north, round Land's End and the Lizard to the gentle slopes of Mount Edgcumbe country park.'
The Western Morning News

THE MOORS OF CORNWALL
by Michael Williams
Contains 77 photographs and drawings. The first ever publication to incorporate the three main moorland areas of Cornwall.
'... is not only a celebration in words of the Moors and their ancient pagan stones and granite strewn tors but a remarkable collection of photographs and drawings of Penwith, Goss and Bodmin Moors...' Sarah Foot, The Editor, Cornish Scene

THE CRUEL CORNISH SEA
by David Mudd. 65 photographs
David Mudd selects more than 30 Cornish shipwrecks, spanning 400 years, in his fascinating account of seas at a coastline that each year claim their toll of human lives.
'This is an important book.' Lord St Levan, The Cornish Times

PEOPLE AND PLACES IN CORNWALL
by Michael Williams
Featuring Sir John Betjeman, Marika Hanbury Tenison, Barbara Hepworth and seven other characters, all of whom contributed richly to the Cornish scene.
'... outlines ten notable characters... whose lives and work have been influenced by "Cornwall's genius to fire creativity"... a fascinating study.' The Cornish Guardian

E.V. THOMPSON'S WESTCOUNTRY
This is a memorable journey: combination of colour and black-and-white photography. Bristol to Land's End happens to be the Bossiney region, and this is precisely E.V. Thompson's Westcountry.
'Stunning photographs and fascinating facts make this an ideal book for South West tourists and residents alike—beautifully atmospheric colour shots make browsing through the pages a real delight.' Jane Leigh, Express & Echo

SEA STORIES OF CORNWALL
by Ken Duxbury. 48 photographs.

'This is a tapestry of true tales', writes the author, 'by no means all of them disasters—which portray something of the spirit, the humour, the tragedy, and the enchantment, that is the lot of we who know the sea.'

'Ken is a sailor, and these stories are written with a close understanding and feel for the incidents.' James Mildren, The Western Morning News

PARANORMAL IN THE WESTCOUNTRY
by Michael Williams

'Michael Williams of Bossiney Books has produced another of his well illustrated books of strange goings-on . . . He explores ghost hunting, healing, psychic painting, tarot cards, mediumship, psycho-expansion, astrology and more.'
Allan Tudor, Herald Express

HISTORIC INNS OF CORNWALL
by Colin Gregory

'. . . charm of this book is that it includes many lesser-known tales of historic hostelries . . . it is not a beer or food guide but a welcome attempt to get down on paper vital aspects of Cornwall's social history.'
John Marquis, The Falmouth Packet

AROUND ST AUSTELL BAY
by Joy Wilson

'. . . Joy Wilson's text is as warm and as sympathetic as the lovely old pictures, making this a book which glows with interest, a soft lamplight shedding illumination on an era dimmed by the passing years. It is a beautiful achievement, and one of the very best in the Bossiney series.' The Western Morning News

WEST CORNWALL IN THE OLD DAYS
by Douglas Williams

St Ives, Mousehole, Newlyn, Penzance, St Just, Helston and Mullion are only some of the places featured in this nostalgic book. Richly illustrated.

'This book has something of a celebratory feel about it. Mr Williams, a Bard of the Cornish Gorsedd, has produced a thoroughly delightful volume, packed with a splendid selection of photographs that span the mid-nineteenth century to the present day. . .' Dr James Whetter, The Cornish Banner

We shall be pleased to send you our catalogue giving full details of our growing list of titles for Devon, Cornwall and Somerset and forthcoming publications.

If you have difficulty in obtaining our titles, write direct to Bossiney Books, Land's End, St Teath, Bodmin, Cornwall.